39 WAYS TO MAKE TRAINING STICK

WHAT TO DO AFTER TRAINEES LEAVE THE ROOM

CHRIS FENNING

39 Ways to Make Training Stick (What to Do After Trainees Leave the Room)

For more about this author please visit www.chrisfenning.com

For permission requests, write to:
Alignment Group Ltd, 20-22 Wenlock Road
London, N1 7GU, United Kingdom
www.chrisfenning.com

Editing by The Pro Book Editor
Interior by IAPS.rocks
Cover Design by 100Covers

eBook ISBN: 978-1-916818-03-3
Paperback ISBN: 978-1-916818-01-9
Hardcover ISBN: 978-1-916818-02-6
Audiobook ISBN: 978-1-916818-04-0

1. Main category—Education / Teaching / Methods & Strategies (EDU029100)
2. Other category—Business & Economics / Education (BUS024000)
3. Other category—Business & Economics / Training (BUS066000)

First Edition

TABLE OF CONTENTS

INTRODUCTION

In the vast world of corporate training, a common lament echoes.

"Why doesn't the training stick?"

Trainers pour hours into crafting the perfect curriculum, students invest their time and energy into attending sessions, and yet, within a few weeks or even days, much of what was learned seems to have evaporated. The cost of this? Frustration, wasted resources, and missed opportunities for the trainer, the trainee, and the organization that set up the training.

Welcome to *39 Ways to Make Training Stick*, a practical guide and toolkit designed specifically for trainers who are passionate about ensuring their training not only educates but also endures. Training is more than just a box to be ticked off. It should be a transformative experience that can empower individuals and reshape organizations. Whether you're a seasoned trainer looking to up your game or a novice just starting out, this book is for you.

Over the years that I have spoken and trained teams in better business communication practices everywhere, from Google to NATO HQ to The Project Management Institute, I've trained more than twenty thousand people and had the privilege of observing, experimenting with, and refining methods to make training more impactful and lasting. Combined with methods used by world class trainers in multiple disciplines and through trial and error, research, and countless feedback sessions, I've distilled these experiences into 39 methods that can help your training sessions leave a more lasting impression than you've achieved in the past.

But why 39 methods? The answer is simple: there is no one-size-fits-all solution. Different audiences, topics, and training environments require different approaches. By offering a diverse set of techniques, this book ensures that you, the trainer, have a rich arsenal at your disposal, ready to be deployed as each situation demands.

Each chapter in this book covers a unique method and provides actionable steps that can be implemented immediately. As you look through these pages, I invite you to approach each method with an open mind. Experiment with them, adapt them to your unique context. I really mean it. The information in this book is a great starting point, but it's designed for you to easily customize these methods to meet your needs. Above all, make sure you observe the results and adapt to make the methods more effective for your students.

The ultimate goal is not just to help learners avoid slipping back into old habits but to ensure they and their companies derive the most possible value from the training investment.

So, are you ready to transform your training sessions from fleeting moments to lasting application? Let's dive in and discover how to truly make training stick.

HOW TO USE THIS BOOK

I DON'T EXPECT ANYONE TO READ this book cover to cover, nor is it likely that you'll use all 39 of these methods. That isn't the intention. Sure, if you'd like to read it all, go right ahead. But, if you don't have the time, you can simply scan the list of methods, find one you like the look of, and jump to that chapter.

This is not a theory book. It is a practical reference to help you find, create, and implement new ways to improve your training, and each of the 39 methods is laid out in the same way so you'll know exactly where to find what you need in each chapter.

However you approach this book, I suggest following these general principles:

1. **Identify Your Needs:** Before diving into the chapters, assess your current training challenges. Are you looking for live, in-person post-training activities? Do you need automated solutions? Is video a good choice? Questions like these will help you focus on the most relevant technique(s) for you and your trainees.
2. **Create Content:** Use the steps of your chosen method to create the content you want to use.
3. **Reuse:** Once created, your "Make Training Stick" content can be reused multiple times. This may be within your company if you're an in-house trainer, or with different clients and cohorts if you are an independent trainer.

4. **Experiment and Adapt:** Not every method will be a perfect fit for every training scenario. Be open to trying out different methods and adapting them to your unique scenarios.
5. **Combine Techniques:** Some methods can be even more effective when combined. As you become familiar with them, consider how they might complement each other.
6. **Feedback Loop:** After implementing a technique, gather feedback from trainees. Their insights will help you refine your approach and choose the most effective methods for future sessions.

Remember, the goal of this book is to provide you with a toolkit. Like any toolkit, it's most effective when you know how and when to use each tool.

CHAPTER STRUCTURE

The first official chapter will outline all 39 ways to make training stick within eight categories that separate the methods by their defining characteristic. The chapters that follow provide the detail for each method within that category.

1. **Description:** This section provides an overview of the method and a summary of how it works.
2. **Creating and Implementing:** Here, you'll find a step-by-step guide on implementing the technique in, or after, your training sessions.
3. **Features of the Technique:** A summary of key features for the method.
    - **Type:** Is the technique an event, activity, resource, or a feedback mechanism?
    - **Frequency:** Is it a one-off or recurring method?
    - **Timing:** When is it best applied—during the training, immediately after, or some time post-training?
    - **Pacing:** Can trainees go at their own pace or is the content scheduled?

- **Real-Time Trainer Input:** Does the training instructor need to be actively involved at the time the method is used?
- **Participation:** Is it designed for individuals or groups?
- **Automation:** Can the technique be automated?
- **Client Facilitation:** Does the method create additional tasks for the company that commissioned the training?
- **Live Event:** Is a live, real-time event needed for the method to succeed?
- **Specialist Tools Needed:** Does the method require specialist tools, software, or other systems to work?

INDEPENDENT VS. IN-HOUSE TRAINERS

Many of the methods in this book involve interactions with trainees after the initial training event is over. If you are an independent trainer, you will need to work with people inside the company that commissioned the training. In some cases, the company may need to take on responsibilities to ensure the success of the approaches. In other cases, part of the service you provide could include leaving them with materials to help them keep the learning momentum going after you've moved onto your next project. This should be discussed with the people arranging the training to ensure support and resources are available and that everyone understands what is required for the ongoing training support to succeed. And what a great value-add to your sales pitch when you can include "making the training stick" efforts and materials.

REUSE, REUSE, REUSE

Almost everything you create for a "Make Training Stick" method can be reused. Don't fall into the trap of thinking you need to start from scratch for each new training session. You may want to tweak elements to fit with specific clients, but generally the content should fit the mindset of "build once, use many times."

Not only can you reuse the content and activities with multiple clients, but it can also be reused with other methods from the book. For example, interactive challenges can be part of a workbook and could also become part of the 3-month calendar and used in flashcards. Parts of the daily email reminders can be used for daily text messages, and so on.

When you create content that helps reinforce the training you give, think about how to reuse it. Maximize the value of everything you create.

EXAMPLES

While it would be great to include examples of each method, it wasn't always practical or possible. Some content doesn't work in book format (e.g., videos and audio), and some of the methods include so much content that they could be a book by themselves (e.g., workbooks and 30-day email sequences).

Wherever possible I've included complete examples, partial examples, or links to view and download examples. If there isn't an example available, you should still be able to create your own content using the step-by-step instructions provided.

Visit www.chrisfenning.com/resources to find and download an up-to-date list of examples.

FINDING KEY CONCEPTS

Most of the methods in this book start with the process of finding the key concepts from the training. If you are unsure of how to do that, there is a step-by-step process at the end of the book to help you easily find that key information to include in your "make it stick" method.

MONITORING AND FEEDBACK

As with all training, it is a good idea to monitor how the process is working and get feedback to improve future versions. Rather than repeat that same guidance in each of the 39 methods, the steps to do them are listed once, here, and you can simply add them to the end of the "Creating and Implementing..." section in each chapter. If specific steps beyond those listed here are needed for feedback and improvement for a particular method, those steps are listed with the method.

Keep in mind, these will require ongoing time commitments from you and/or representatives from the organization that arranged the training. Make sure you consider this when planning the training.

Add the following steps to the end of the "Creating and Implementing..." section in each chapter as needed:

Encourage Feedback

- Ask participants for feedback on the method with the goal of understanding whether they found it helpful and engaging. Any weaknesses learners share with you are good indicators of areas to improve in future training.

Monitor Engagement

- If possible, track metrics like video views, completion rates, and any interactive elements to assess engagement. This data can provide insights into whether trainees are interactive with the content. Low interaction levels may mean you need to try a different method for that training topic or find a way to improve the open rates.

Update as Needed

- As training content evolves or is updated, ensure that the method is also revised to stay current so participants always have access to the most up-to-date refresher content.

Monitor Progress

- Set up a system to track trainees' progress over time. This could be a digital platform, regular check-ins, or feedback sessions. Encourage trainees to share their experiences, challenges, and achievements.

Celebrate Achievements

- Recognize and celebrate the milestones and achievements of trainees. This could be through certificates, awards, or simply acknowledgment in group settings and can be done by you in subsequent training sessions or by the client organization in their team meetings.

THE 39 WAYS

To make it easier to get started, I've arranged the methods into categories. Some methods fit into more than one category, but to avoid duplication, they are only listed in the most appropriate one.

REMINDERS & REINFORCEMENT TOOLS

These methods provide additional scheduled content to the trainees after the main event.

1. **3-Month Plan:** Structured Reinforcement for Long-Term Retention
2. **Animated Recap Videos:** Visual Refreshers for Lasting Retention
3. **Learning Calendars:** Daily Doses of Learning and Reflection
4. **Daily Tip Texts:** Bite-Sized Reinforcement for Continuous Learning
5. **Email Tips Sequence:** Sustained Learning Through Consistent Digital Touchpoints
6. **Integration with Daily Work:** Making Training a Part of Everyday Tasks
7. **Multimedia Messages:** Engaging reminders on their phones
8. **Themed Newsletters:** Deepening Learning Through Monthly Focus

9. **Video reminders – Impromptu:** A Personalized Approach to Reinforcing Training
10. **Video reminders – Scheduled:** A Reinforcement Strategy for Long-Term Retention

ACTIVITIES

Activities are engaging and make a change from the passive receipt of reminders. Choose from the following activity types to shift your trainees from theory to application.

11. **Challenges:** Engaging Trainees Through Competitive Learning
12. **Follow-Up Actions – Trainee Defined:** Personal Commitments for Tangible Implementation
13. **Follow-Up Actions – Trainer Defined:** Structured Steps for Immediate Application
14. **Interactive Email Challenges:** Engaging Trainees Beyond the Classroom
15. **Participant-Generated Content:** Empowering Trainees to Become Contributors
16. **Quiz Series:** Gamified Recall and Reinforcement
17. **Storytelling Series:** Harnessing the Power of Narrative
18. **Teach Someone Else:** The Power of Peer-to-Peer Knowledge Transfer

RECOGNITION & REWARD

If you want to reward trainees for the application of what they learned, try these methods.

19. **Digital Badges & Certifications:** Recognizing and Rewarding Skill Application
20. **Digital Stickers:** Fun and Engaging Training Reminders
21. **Recognition & Reward:** Celebrating Application and Mastery

LIVE EVENTS

Live events provide opportunities to share, learn, and reinforce the training. To add some human interaction to your training support, try these methods.

22. **Follow-Up Sessions:** Reinforcing Learning Through Scheduled Revisits
23. **Ongoing Support:** Continuous Learning Through Immediate Assistance
24. **Virtual Hangouts:** A Collaborative Approach to Reinforcing Training

SELF-PACED

Not everything has to run on a schedule. To help those who prefer to learn at their own pace, try these methods.

25. **Card Deck Activities:** Tangible Reminders for Skill Mastery
26. **Digital Flashcards:** Reinforcing Training Principles with Real-Life Context
27. **Digital Resources:** On-Demand Reinforcement for Continuous Learning
28. **Workbooks:** Interactive Guides for Sustained Engagement and Reflection
29. **Interactive Augmented Reality (AR) Posters:** Immersive Reminders in the Workplace
30. **Podcast Series:** Amplifying Training Through Engaging Audio Content
31. **QR Codes:** Bridging the Gap Between Training and Application
32. **Training Application Diaries:** A Journey of Reflection and Growth

COMMUNITY COLLABORATION

Learning is easier within a community. Provide opportunities for accountability and support with these community-focused methods.

33. **Accountability Buddies:** A Partnership in Learning and Growth
34. **Collaborative Online Boards:** Harnessing Collective Wisdom for Enhanced Learning
35. **Peer Learning Groups:** Harnessing Collective Wisdom

REAL-TIME FEEDBACK

Giving feedback and support at the moment the training is applied helps trainees start off on the right path and stay there.

36. **Feedback Mechanism:** Continuous Learning Through Constructive Insights
37. **Real-Time Feedback Tools:** Immediate Insights for Continuous Improvement
38. **AI Powered Tools:** Tailored Reinforcement Through Intelligent Analysis

CUSTOMIZED SOLUTIONS

Not every situation can use a prepared solution. Sometimes you'll need to create a custom solution for a unique set of circumstances.

39. **Custom Follow-Up:** Tailored Reinforcement for Optimal Training Outcomes

REMINDERS & REINFORCEMENT TOOLS

This section focuses on methods that deliver additional scheduled content to trainees after the main event to ensure the lessons learned do not fade from memory. These methods are designed to be built once and used repeatedly. Each one includes a level of automation, and in some cases, the entire method can be delivered automatically after initial setup.

As you delve into the methods detailed in this section, think of them as your toolkit for crafting a learning journey that extends beyond the classroom. You don't need to use every method. Just pick the one or two that best fit the training topic, the learners, and the situation.

1. **3-Month Plan:** Structured Reinforcement for Long-Term Retention
2. **Animated Recap Videos:** Visual Refreshers for Lasting Retention
3. **Learning Calendars:** Daily Doses of Learning and Reflection
4. **Daily Tip Texts:** Bite-Sized Reinforcement for Continuous Learning
5. **Email Tips Sequence:** Sustained Learning Through Consistent Digital Touchpoints
6. **Integration with Daily Work:** Making Training a Part of Everyday Tasks
7. **Multimedia Messages:** Engaging reminders on their phones

8. **Themed Newsletters:** Deepening Learning Through Monthly Focus
9. **Video reminders – Impromptu:** A Personalized Approach to Reinforcing Training
10. **Video reminders – Scheduled:** A Reinforcement Strategy for Long-Term Retention

CASE STUDY

After completing a comprehensive training program for their employees on new software protocols, the trainers at Peritum did not simply close their manuals and consider their job done. Instead, they implemented a 3-month plan that provided structured, ongoing reinforcement. Automated emails and Slack messages delivered tips, reminders, and animated recap videos that broke down complex concepts into short, engaging summaries. Trainees were not expected to remember everything they had been taught but were assisted with regular, yet not overwhelming reminders and reinforcement.

The result? Six months post-training, employees had not only retained the knowledge but were applying it consistently and efficiently in their daily work. Peritum's story is a testament to the power of reminders and reinforcement tools.

3-MONTH PLAN

STRUCTURED REINFORCEMENT FOR LONG-TERM RETENTION

At the end of the primary training session, give your trainees a structured schedule of daily, weekly, and monthly activities spread over three months. Instead of relying solely on a single training event, this method extends the learning journey, breaking it down into daily, weekly, and monthly tasks and challenges that turn information into actions and new habits. This uses the psychological principles of spaced repetition and active recall to help trainees remember, understand, and apply what they learn.

1. **Daily Tasks:** These should be short, focused activities designed to easily fit into the trainee's daily routine. They might include quick quizzes, reading short articles, or practicing a specific skill.
2. **Weekly Challenges:** A bit more involved than daily tasks, these challenges should aim to consolidate the learning from the daily tasks that week and add an extra level of reinforcement. Examples might include role-playing exercises, group discussions, or application of the training content in real-world scenarios.
3. **Monthly Milestones:** These are more comprehensive activities designed to review and consolidate the learning from the entire month. They could be in the form of assessments, presentations, or group projects.

4. **Feedback Loops:** Throughout the three months, integrate mechanisms for feedback (e.g., peer review, 1:1 or group feedback, tests, etc.) so trainees can reflect on their progress, understand areas of improvement, and seek clarification on any doubts.

CREATING AND IMPLEMENTING "THE 3-MONTH PLAN" METHOD

Step 1 – Identify Core Objectives: Review the training content to pinpoint key learning objectives you want trainees to achieve by the end of the three months. Prioritize these objectives based on their importance and complexity.

Step 2 – Break Down Objectives: Segment the objectives into smaller, actionable tasks or activities that align with the daily, weekly, or monthly schedule in terms of complexity and time commitment.

Step 3 – Design Daily Activities: Create a list of short, focused tasks for each day, making sure they are varied to keep engagement high (e.g., reading, practicing a skill, reflection). Incorporate real-world application wherever possible.

Step 4 – Design Weekly Activities: Develop more in-depth tasks that consolidate the daily activities. Consider including group discussions, mini-projects, or mentorship sessions. Schedule a specific day of the week for these activities, ensuring consistency.

Step 5 – Design Monthly Milestones: Plan comprehensive sessions or activities for each month. These could be workshops, deep-dive sessions, or project presentations. Ensure they provide opportunities for feedback, reflection, and assessment of progress.

Step 6 – Compile Resources: Gather or create any resources trainees will need to complete the activities, such as reading materials, tools, quizzes, software, etc. Ensure resources are easily accessible, either through a shared platform or physical distribution.

Step 7 – Create a Clear Roadmap: Design a visually appealing and easy-to-follow plan that outlines the daily, weekly, and monthly

activities. Include clear instructions, deadlines, and any necessary resources for each task.

Step 8 – Communicate the Plan: Introduce the 3-Month Plan toward the end of the main training session. Explain its purpose, benefits, and how it will support their learning journey. Distribute the roadmap to all trainees, either digitally or in print.

Step 9 – Monitor Progress: Set up a system to track trainees' progress. This could be a digital platform, regular check-ins, or feedback sessions. Encourage trainees to share their experiences, challenges, and achievements. (NOTE: You can do this, OR you can arrange for the client organization to lead this.)

Step 10 – Celebrate Achievements: Recognize and celebrate the milestones and achievements of trainees. This could be through certificates, awards, or simply acknowledgment in group settings.

FEATURES OF THE TECHNIQUE

Type	Resource
Frequency	One-off
Timing	Immediately after the training
Pacing	Self-pace
Real-Time Trainer Input	No
Participation	Individual
Automation	No
Client Facilitation	Optional
Live Event	No
Specialist Tools Needed	No

EXAMPLE

This example shows month one of a 3-month plan to support a business-to-business (B2B) sales training workshop. It isn't a day-by-day calendar, but rather, each task is repeated over multiple days to use the power of repetition to reinforce and practice. You

could create a calendar with different activities on each day if it adds value to the trainees. The format of this month can be repeated, with different activities, for the remainder of the 3-month calendar.

MONTH 1: FOUNDATIONS OF B2B SALES

Daily Activities: (weekdays only, no activities on weekends)

- **Week 1:** Study a different B2B sales model each day, noting its strengths and weaknesses.
- **Week 2:** Dedicate 15 minutes daily to practicing elevator pitches for different products/services.
- **Week 3:** Research and identify key decision-makers in various industries.
- **Week 4:** Role-play cold calls with peers.

Weekly Activities:

- **Week 1:** Attend a workshop on understanding B2B buyer personas.
- **Week 2:** Join a webinar on the latest B2B sales tools and technologies.
- **Week 3:** Collaborate with a team to map out a typical B2B sales cycle.
- **Week 4:** Seek feedback on your product knowledge from a product manager or expert.

Monthly Milestones:

- **End of Month:** Conduct a mock sales presentation for a potential high-value client, incorporating the month's learnings.

ANIMATED RECAP VIDEOS

VISUAL REFRESHERS FOR LASTING RETENTION

Use animation platforms to create short, engaging recap videos of training modules. These can be sent out intermittently as refreshers. Instead of relying on lengthy documents or slides for revision, turn key takeaways from training modules into concise, engaging visual narratives.

1. **Content Distillation:** Identify the core concepts, insights, and takeaways from the training module that need reinforcement.
2. **Script Creation:** Create a concise script, focusing on simplifying complex ideas into easily digestible chunks suitable for animation. Keep it short, typically from 2 to 5 minutes per video.
3. **Animation Design:** Bring the script to life using animation platforms or software. This can involve creating characters, scenarios, and visual metaphors that depict the training's context in a resonating way.
4. **Voiceover and Sound:** Add a clear voiceover that guides viewers through the recap. Background music and sound effects can further elevate the viewing experience.

5. **Distribution:** Share the completed videos with trainees via email, integrated into Learning Management Systems (LMS), or even shared on company intranets. To ensure continuous reinforcement, these videos can be sent out intermittently, serving as periodic refreshers.

CREATING AND IMPLEMENTING ANIMATED RECAP VIDEOS

Step 1 – Identify Key Takeaways: Review the training content and pinpoint the most important points or concepts that participants should retain. Condense these points into bite-sized, easily digestible chunks suitable for animation.

Step 2 – Choose an Animation Platform: Research and select an animation platform or software that suits your needs. Ensure the chosen platform aligns with your technical expertise and budget. If you or your team don't have the expertise to create your own videos, look for freelancers to do this for you.

Step 3 – Script the Recap: Write a concise script for the animated video, ensuring it covers the key takeaways in an engaging way. Keep the language simple and direct to make it easily understandable.

Step 4 – Design the Animation (Outsourcing Optional): Use the animation platform to bring your script to life by incorporating visuals that complement and reinforce the content. Characters, props, and scenarios should relate to the training's context.

Step 5 – Add Voiceover (Outsourcing Optional): Record a clear voiceover to accompany the animation. Alternatively, use background music and on-screen text to convey the message. If using music and text, make the script accessible for people with visual or hearing difficulties.

Step 6 – Test the Video: Before finalizing, show the animated recap to a small group for feedback. Make necessary adjustments based on their input to ensure clarity and effectiveness.

Step 7 – Finalize and Export (Outsourcing Optional): Once satisfied, finalize the animation and export it in a format suitable for sharing, such as MP4.

Step 8 – Distribute the Recap Videos: Share the animated recap videos with participants by sharing a video link via email, company intranet, or a Learning Management System (LMS). Consider scheduling the release of these videos intermittently (e.g., a week after the training, a month after, and so on) to serve as periodic refreshers.

Step 9 – Monitor Engagement Metrics: If possible, track metrics like video views, completion rates, and any interactive elements to understand trainee engagement. This data can provide insights into the video's effectiveness and areas for improvement. (e.g., drop-off rates show when trainees stop watching a video)

FEATURES OF THE TECHNIQUE

Type	Resource
Frequency	Over time after the training
Timing	Recurring
Pacing	Self-paced
Real-Time Trainer Input	No
Participation	Individual
Automation	Yes
Client Facilitation	Optional
Live Event	No
Specialist Tools Needed	Yes, to create and possibly for distribution and tracking

LEARNING CALENDARS

DAILY DOSES OF LEARNING AND REFLECTION

SHARE A MONTHLY CALENDAR THAT gives trainees a roadmap of continuous learning and reflection. Each day, week, or month should be dedicated to a specific topic or concept from the training, accompanied by a brief activity or reflection prompt. This helps trainees engage with the training material consistently, but in manageable chunks, making the learning process both sustainable and effective.

1. **Calendar Creation:** A post-training calendar that has each day, week, or month assigned a specific theme or topic from the training content.
2. **Activity or Reflection Prompts:** Alongside each theme, a brief activity or reflection prompt could be a mini challenge, a question, a quick exercise, or even a short reading recommendation.
3. **Distribution:** Sharing the calendar could be done in a digital format (like a shared Google Calendar or a downloadable PDF) or a physical printout.
4. **Daily Engagement:** Trainees engage with the calendar daily, diving into the theme of the day and completing the associated activity or reflection.

5. **Feedback Mechanism:** Optionally, a platform or forum can be set up where trainees share their reflections, experiences, or any questions arising from the daily themes.
6. **Monthly Recap:** At the end of the month, a group session can be organized to discuss the month's themes, share experiences, and address any overarching questions or challenges.

CREATING AND IMPLEMENTING "THE LEARNING CALENDAR" METHOD

Step 1 – Content Breakdown: Review the training content and list the key topics, concepts, or skills participants need to master.

Step 2 – Calendar Design: Choose a monthly calendar template. This can be digital (e.g., Google Calendar, Microsoft Outlook) or a printable design. Assign each day, week, and month a specific theme or topic from your list.

Step 3 – Craft Daily and Weekly Prompts: For each day or week's theme, create a brief activity or reflection prompt. This could be a question, a mini challenge, a quick exercise, or a short reading snippet. Ensure the prompts are varied to keep engagement levels high throughout the month.

Step 4 – Enhance with Visuals (Optional): Add relevant images, icons, or visual cues to each day to make the calendar more engaging and visually appealing.

Step 5 – Distribution: Share the completed calendar with the trainees. If digital, provide access links or share directly. If physical, distribute printed copies. Ensure trainees understand how to use the calendar and the importance of daily engagement.

Step 6 – Set Up a Feedback Platform (Optional): Create a platform or forum where trainees can share their daily reflections, experiences, or questions. This could be a dedicated chat group, an online forum, or monthly meetings.

Step 7 – Daily Reminders (Optional): To boost engagement, consider sending daily reminders or notifications to trainees, nudging them to check the day's theme and complete the prompt.

FEATURES OF THE TECHNIQUE

Type	Reminder
Frequency	Recurring
Timing	Over time after the training
Pacing	Scheduled
Real-Time Trainer Input	No
Participation	Individual
Automation	Yes
Client Facilitation	Optional
Live Event	No
Specialist Tools Needed	No

EXAMPLE

Here is an example of one month from a "Learn Intermediate Microsoft Excel" learning calendar. The training taught more advanced functions in Excel than most people are familiar with. Learners improved the speed and accuracy of data processed in Excel in their day-to-day work. Each day in the learning calendar has a tip and either a question, activity, or reading recommendation. Over the course of the 3-months, learners are repeatedly exposed to the techniques from the course and the repetition helps with both recall and application.

Monday	Tuesday	Wednesday	Thursday	Friday
2	3	4	5	6
Tip: VLOOKUP only looks to the right. For more flexibility, consider INDEX & MATCH. **Activity:** Create a VLOOKUP formula to retrieve data from a table. Can you replicate the same result using INDEX & MATCH?	**Question**: Why might you use absolute references in Excel formulas? **Activity:** Create a formula using both relative and absolute references. Copy it down a column and observe the difference.	**Reading Recommendation**: "Excel Formulas & Functions For Dummies" by Ken Bluttman. Focus on the chapter about logical functions. **Activity:** After reading, create a nested IF formula to categorize sales data	**Tip**: SUMIF and COUNTIF are powerful for conditional aggregation. **Activity:** Use SUMIF to total sales for a specific region. How does this change when using COUNTIF?	**Question**: What is the order of operations in Excel, and why is it important? **Activity:** Create a complex formula that combines multiplication, addition and parentheses. Test different scenarios.
9	10	11	12	13
Tip: Errors like #N/A can be handled using IFERROR. **Activity:** Create a VLOOKUP formula that uses IFERROR to display "Not Found" when data is missing.	**Reading Recommendation**: Explore Excel's official documentation on date and time functions. **Activity:** Calculate the number of days between your birthdate and today using DATEDIF().	**Tip**: "Remove Duplicates" is essential for data cleaning. **Question**: In what scenarios might duplicate data entries be problematic?	**Reading Recommendation**: "Excel 2019 Bible" by Michael Alexander, Richard Kusleika. Focus on the chapter about data management. **Activity:** After reading, apply filters to a dataset to view rows based on multiple criteria.	**Tip**: Data can be sorted by multiple columns. **Activity:** Sort a dataset first by product category and then by sales figures in descending order.
16	17	18	19	20
Tip: Data validation restricts cell input. **Question**: Why might you use a drop-down list in a spreadsheet?	**Tip**: PivotTables need refreshing if source data changes. **Activity:** Update the source data and refresh the PivotTable. Observe the changes.	**Tip**: "Text to Columns" splits data into multiple columns. **Activity:** Split a column with full addresses into separate columns for street, city, state, and zip code.	**Tip**: "Flash Fill" recognizes patterns. **Activity:** Type a series of first names in column A. In column B, type the first name with its initial letter capitalized. Start using "Flash Fill" to complete the rest.	**Reading Recommendation**: Explore online forums like Stack Overflow for Excel tips on data management.
23	24	25	26	27
Tip: Ensure data is in a tabular format for PivotTables. **Question**: Why are PivotTables useful for large datasets?	**Reading Recommendation**: Explore Excel's official documentation on PivotTable calculated fields. **Activity:** Prepare a dataset and create a basic PivotTable.	**Reading Recommendation**: "Excel PivotTables and PivotCharts: Your visual blueprint for creating dynamic spreadsheets" by Paul McFedries. **Activity:** After reading, change a sum aggregation in a PivotTable to an average.	**Tip**: Slicers make PivotTables interactive. **Activity:** Add a slicer to a PivotTable. Filter data using the slicer and observe how the PivotTable updates.	**Tip**: "Show Values As" offers different data display options. **Activity:** Display data in a PivotTable as a percentage of the column total.

DAILY TIP TEXTS

BITE-SIZED REINFORCEMENT FOR CONTINUOUS LEARNING

SEND DAILY OR WEEKLY TEXT messages containing concise, actionable tips related to the training topic. When trainees receive regular reminders that not only refresh their memory but also guide them in applying their knowledge in real-world contexts, it ensures that the training content remains top-of-mind and can be more regularly applied.

1. **Content Curation:** After the main training session, curate a list of bite-sized tips that encapsulate key points, best practices, or actionable insights from the training content.
2. **Message Platform Integration:** Use a text message platform or service that allows for scheduled text message broadcasts to a list of recipients. Ensure compliance with privacy regulations and obtain consent from trainees to receive these messages.
3. **Schedule and Frequency:** Decide on the frequency of the texts, whether daily or weekly. Schedule the messages in a sequence that logically builds on the training content, ensuring a smooth flow of information.
4. **Crafting the Message:** Each message should be concise, typically not exceeding 160 characters. The message should be clear, actionable, and relevant to the trainees' daily tasks or challenges.

5. **Feedback Loop (Optional):** Include prompts for feedback or questions in the text message, encouraging trainees to engage and share their experiences or challenges. This requires active involvement and moderation from the trainer or a group message option where people can interact with each other.
6. **Duration:** Determine the duration of this method, which could range from a few weeks to several months depending on the depth and complexity of the training content.

CREATING AND IMPLEMENTING "DAILY TIP TEXTS" METHOD

Step 1 – Content Identification: Review the main training content to identify key points, best practices, and actionable insights that can be transformed into bite-sized tips.

Step 2 – Message Crafting: Write concise text messages for each tip, ensuring they are clear, actionable, and typically not exceeding 160 characters.

Step 3 – Obtain Consent: Before sending any messages, ensure you have the consent of each trainee to receive text message notifications. This is crucial for privacy and regulatory compliance.

Step 4 – Choose a Text Message Platform: Select a reliable text message broadcasting platform or service that allows for scheduled messages. Ensure it can handle the volume of messages and recipients you're planning for.

Step 5 – Upload Recipient List: Add the list of trainee phone numbers to the platform, ensuring that data is secure and protected.

Step 6 – Decide on the Schedule: Decide on the frequency (daily or weekly) and set a timeline for how long you'll send these tips.

Step 7 – Set Up the Message System: Upload or create the messages in your chosen message platform. Arrange the messages in a logical sequence that builds on the training content. Configure the platform to send the messages on the schedule you have defined.

Step 8 – Monitor Delivery: Regularly check the broadcasting platform to ensure messages are being delivered successfully. Address any delivery failures or issues promptly; otherwise, trainees may disengage and ignore any news messages when the delivery restarts.

Step 9 – Encourage Feedback: Periodically, include prompts in the messages for feedback or questions. This not only fosters engagement but also helps you gauge the effectiveness of the tips.

Step 10 – Analyze Engagement: Use the broadcasting platform's analytics to monitor engagement. Track metrics like delivery rates, open rates, and any feedback received.

Step 11 – Conclude the Series: Once the scheduled series of tips is complete, send a concluding message thanking trainees for their engagement and providing guidance on next steps or further resources.

FEATURES OF THE TECHNIQUE

Type	Reminder
Frequency	Recurring
Timing	Over time after the training
Pacing	Self-pace
Real-Time Trainer Input	No
Participation	Individual
Automation	Yes
Client Facilitation	No
Live Event	No
Specialist Tools Needed	Yes

EXAMPLE

These daily text tips and reminders are from a short course on mastering meetings at work. The company had a history of meetings overrunning, including more people than necessary, and not producing valuable outputs. The tip texts were delivered at the start of the workday and prompted the trainees to check that any meetings they had that day were well planned.

Day 1: 📅 Tip: Start every meeting with a clear agenda that sets the tone and direction.

Day 2: ⏰ Tip: Respect everyone's time. Always start and end meetings punctually.

Day 3: 🎤 Tip: Encourage participation. Ask open-ended questions to engage quieter members.

Day 4: 💡 Tip: End with clear action items. Assign tasks with deadlines to keep momentum.

Day 5: 🔄 Tip: Regularly review meeting effectiveness. Are they too long? Too frequent? Adjust accordingly.

EMAIL TIPS SEQUENCE

SUSTAINED LEARNING THROUGH CONSISTENT DIGITAL TOUCHPOINTS

The Email Tips Sequence provides trainees with consistent, bite-sized reinforcements of training content through key concepts, actionable tips, and reminders delivered directly to their inboxes. Start with a daily cadence for an initial period (e.g., 1 – 3 months) and transition to weekly reminders for the remainder of the year if preferred. This method helps keep the training content top-of-mind and increases the chances that it is applied.

1. **Content Creation:** Develop a series of concise, actionable tips or reminders based on the training's key concepts. The more practical these are and the closer they relate to the work the trainees do, the better.
2. **Email Platform Selection:** Choose an email marketing platform or automation tool that supports drip campaigns, such as Mailchimp, SendinBlue, or HubSpot.
3. **Sequence Setup:** Configure the email sequence starting with daily emails for the initial period (1 – 3 months) and then transitioning to weekly emails. Ensure each email is timed appropriately and spaced out to avoid overwhelming recipients.

4. **Personalization:** Where possible, personalize the emails to address the trainee by name or reference specific training sessions they attended to increase engagement and relevance.
5. **Engagement Elements:** Incorporate interactive elements in the emails, such as clickable links to additional resources, quizzes, or feedback forms.
6. **Opt-In Process:** While the initial idea is to sign up all participants, it's essential to ensure they have the option to opt out at any point. This respects their preferences and complies with email marketing regulations.
7. **Monitoring and Analytics:** Use the analytics provided by the email platform to track open rates, click-through rates, unsubscribes, and any feedback. This data can offer insights into the effectiveness of the email sequence and areas for improvement.

CREATING AND IMPLEMENTING "THE EMAIL TIPS SEQUENCE" METHOD

Step 1 – Content Development: Review the training material to extract key concepts, actionable tips, and reminders that can be conveyed in concise email formats.

Step 2 – Choose an Email Platform: Select an email marketing or automation platform that supports drip campaigns. Platforms like Mailchimp, SendinBlue, or HubSpot are popular choices. If working with a client, they may have an internal email platform you can use.

Step 3 – Design the Emails (Outsourcing Optional): Create visually appealing email templates that are mobile-responsive. Ensure they align with your or your client's branding and comply with accessibility and diversity, equity, and inclusion (DEI) best practices.

Step 4 – Sequence Structuring: Plan the sequence of emails. Start with daily emails for the initial period (between 1 and 3 months), followed by weekly emails for the remainder of the year.

Step 5 – Personalization: Integrate features that allow for personalization to speak directly to each person receiving it and make each email seem less generic. Use automation and mail-merge tools to do small things such as addressing the trainee by name or referencing specific sessions they attended.

Step 6 – Add Interactive Elements: Embed links to additional resources, quizzes, feedback forms, or other interactive components to enhance engagement.

Step 7 – Opt-In/Opt-Out Mechanisms: While enrolling participants, ensure they are informed and have the option to opt out. Include clear unsubscribe options in every email to comply with email marketing regulations.

Step 8 – Launch the Campaign: Enroll trainees in the email sequence. Ensure they receive a welcome email explaining the purpose and frequency of the upcoming email campaign.

FEATURES OF THE TECHNIQUE

Type	Reminder
Frequency	Recurring
Timing	Over time after the training
Pacing	Scheduled
Real-Time Trainer Input	No
Participation	Individual
Automation	Yes
Client Facilitation	Optional
Live Event	No
Specialist Tools Needed	Yes

EXAMPLE

Here is an example email from the middle of a sequence about running successful meetings. The email is short, refers to the training, and has a simple call to action for the reader.

> **Subject:** Step 9 – Stay Agile in Meetings
>
> **Introduction:** Hello [NAME],
>
> Step number nine of our successful meetings series is here, emphasizing the need for adaptability in meetings.
>
> **Key Point:** To ensure meetings are productive, do these four things:
>
> 1. *Define the goal.* Start with a clear desired output.
> 2. *Stay observant.* Monitor the conversation's trajectory and its alignment with the goal.
> 3. *Be decisive.* If the conversation deviates, decide whether to return to the original goal or adapt to a new one.
> 4. *Keep everyone informed.* Ensure all participants are aware of any changes in direction.
>
> **Next Steps:** During your next meeting, stay alert for deviations and be open to adjustments. By ensuring everyone is on the same page, you'll make the most of your time together.
>
> Keep an eye out for Step 10 later this week. Until then, have great meetings!
>
> All the best,
>
> Chris

INTEGRATION WITH DAILY WORK

MAKING TRAINING A PART OF EVERYDAY TASKS

INSTEAD OF TREATING TRAINING AS a separate entity or an isolated event, this method updates or adds training support into the daily work of the trainees. For instance, if the training is about a new software tool, a checklist for the use of this tool can pop up when the tool is opened each day. This ensures that the knowledge and skills acquired are immediately and consistently applied in the real-world context of a trainee's job. This approach requires a good understanding of the trainee's work and collaboration with the organization they work for to ensure the right type of support is given. It is important not to add unnecessary steps to the burden of their daily work.

1. **Task Analysis:** Analyze the daily tasks and responsibilities of the trainees and identify areas where the training content can be applied.
2. **Practical Application:** Design the training content in a way that directly correlates with these daily tasks. Use real-world examples, scenarios, and exercises that mirror their job functions.
3. **Embedding Techniques:** Post-training, provide trainees with tools, templates, or checklists that integrate the training content into their tasks.

4. **Regular Check-Ins:** Schedule regular check-ins with trainees to discuss the integration process. Address any challenges they face and provide guidance on how to better embed the training into their tasks.
5. **Continuous Reinforcement:** Offer additional resources, such as quick reference guides, tutorials, or mentorship programs to support trainees as they apply their training in their daily tasks.

CREATING AND IMPLEMENTING "INTEGRATION WITH DAILY WORK" METHOD

Step 1 – Role Analysis: Begin by understanding the roles and responsibilities of the trainees. This might involve job shadowing, interviews, or reviewing job descriptions.

Step 2 – Identify Integration Points: Pinpoint specific tasks or areas in their daily work where the training content can be directly applied.

Step 3 – Design Contextual Training: Tailor the training content to align with these integration points. Use real-world examples and scenarios that mirror the trainees' daily tasks.

Step 4 – Create Integration Tools: Develop tools or resources that can aid in the integration process. This could be checklists, templates, or quick reference guides that embed the training content into daily tasks.

Step 5 – Conduct the Training: Deliver the training, emphasizing the direct application to daily tasks. Ensure trainees understand not just the *what* but also the *how* of integrating their learning.

Step 6 – Post-Training Support: Provide trainees with the integration tools and resources and offer additional support, such as tutorials, mentorship, or help desks, to assist them in the initial stages of integration.

FEATURES OF THE TECHNIQUE

Type	Activity
Frequency	Recurring
Timing	Over time after the training
Pacing	Self-pace
Real-Time Trainer Input	No
Participation	Individual
Automation	No
Client Facilitation Required	Yes
Live Event	No
Specialist Tools Needed	Possibly

MULTIMEDIA MESSAGES

ENGAGING REMINDERS ON THEIR PHONES

SEND OUT ENGAGING MULTIMEDIA-RICH REMINDERS that are bite-sized and relevant and entertaining. Formats can range from short voice notes explaining a tip, video clips of the training concept in action, or even GIFs and memes that humorously remind participants of common uses or mistakes connected to the learning concepts. This method offers a regular and often entertaining way to keep training content fresh in the minds of trainees.

1. **Platform Selection:** Choose a messaging platform that's widely used among your trainees. Platforms like WhatsApp, Telegram, or Slack are popular choices due to their multimedia support and widespread adoption.
2. **Content Creation:** Develop a series of multimedia reminders tailored to the training's key points. This could be:
   - Voice notes summarizing essential concepts.
   - Short video clips showcasing real-life applications or demonstrations.
   - GIFs or memes that humorously highlight common mistakes or reinforce best practices.

3. **Scheduled Delivery:** Use the platform's scheduling feature (if available) or set reminders to periodically send out these multimedia messages. The frequency can be daily, weekly, or even monthly, depending on the training's depth and complexity.
4. **Interactive Engagement:** Encourage trainees to respond to these messages, fostering a two-way communication channel. They can share their experiences, ask questions, or even contribute their own multimedia insights.

CREATING AND IMPLEMENTING "MULTIMEDIA MESSAGES" METHOD

Step 1 – Platform Selection: Survey participants or assess company usage to determine the most popular and accessible messaging platform (e.g., WhatsApp, Telegram, Slack). Ensure the chosen platform supports the multimedia formats you intend to use.

Step 2 – Content Planning: Review the training material to identify key points and concepts that would benefit from multimedia reinforcement. Decide on the types of multimedia (voice notes, videos, GIFs, memes) that best convey each point.

Step 3 – Content Creation: Record clear and concise voice notes or video clips. Ensure good audio and visual quality. Source or create relevant GIFs and memes. Ensure they are appropriate and align with the training's tone. Store all multimedia content in an organized folder for easy access.

Step 4 – Set a Schedule: Determine the frequency of sending out multimedia messages, either daily, weekly, or monthly, and create a content calendar outlining which multimedia message will be sent on which date.

Step 5 – Platform Setup: Create a group or channel on the chosen platform, specifically for training reminders. Add all training participants to the group or channel.

Step 6 – Message Delivery: Begin sending out multimedia messages according to your content calendar. If the platform supports scheduling, set up automated message deliveries. Otherwise, set reminders for manual sending.

Step 7 – Foster Interaction: Encourage participants to engage with the content. Ask open-ended questions or set mini challenges related to the multimedia content. Promote a positive and open environment where trainees can share their experiences, questions, or insights.

FEATURES OF THE TECHNIQUE

Type	Reminder
Frequency	Recurring
Timing	Over time after the training
Pacing	Scheduled
Real-Time Trainer Input	No
Participation	Individual
Automation	Yes
Client Facilitation	No
Live Event	No
Specialist Tools Needed	Yes

THEMED NEWSLETTERS

DEEPENING LEARNING THROUGH MONTHLY FOCUS

Create and send a monthly newsletter focused on a different aspect or theme from the training each month. The newsletter could contain articles, activities, quizzes, and real-life anecdotes from participants about their experiences in applying the techniques. Rather than bombarding participants with a deluge of information all at once, this method breaks down the training content into digestible chunks, revisiting each aspect in depth over time.

1. **Content Curation:** Each month, select a particular theme or topic from the training, then populate the newsletter with a variety of content types—articles, activities, quizzes, and real-life anecdotes—all centered around the theme. Wherever possible, reuse existing content and images from the training. These can be edited to fit the desired length for the newsletter.
2. **Participant Involvement:** Encourage participants to contribute their own experiences, challenges, and success stories, investing them in the process and making the newsletter more relatable and engaging. This peer sharing can inspire others and provide diverse perspectives on applying the training in real-world scenarios.

3. **Regular Distribution:** Send the newsletter out at regular intervals, typically monthly, ensuring that participants receive consistent reminders and reinforcements of the training material.
4. **Interactive Elements:** Incorporate quizzes and activities so participants are not just passive consumers of the content but actively engaging with the material, testing their knowledge and applying what they've learned.

CREATING AND IMPLEMENTING "THEMED NEWSLETTERS"

Step 1 – Content Mapping: Review the training material and break it down into distinct themes or topics that can each be the focus of a monthly newsletter.

Step 2 – Content Schedule: Develop a content calendar that outlines which theme will be covered in each month's newsletter for the designated period.

Step 3 – Design the Newsletter Template: Create a visually appealing and easy-to-read template for the newsletter. Ensure there are sections for articles, quizzes, activities, and participant anecdotes.

Step 4 – Source Content: Begin with the first theme on your schedule.

- Write or source relevant articles.
- Design quizzes or activities.
- Collect real-life anecdotes from participants (consider sending out a monthly call for stories related to the theme).

Step 5 – Engage with Participants: Encourage participants to contribute by sharing their experiences, challenges, and success stories related to the monthly theme. This can be done through emails, internal platforms, or during follow-up sessions.

Step 6 – Compile and Edit: Gather all the content for the month and fit it into the newsletter template. Ensure the content flows logically and is free of errors.

Step 7 – Distribution: Use email marketing tools or internal communication platforms to send out the newsletter to all participants.

Step 8 – Feedback Loop: At the end of each newsletter, include a feedback form or link. This will help you gauge the effectiveness of the content and make necessary adjustments for future editions.

Step 9 – Integrate with Other Training Methods: If you're using other post-training methods, consider integrating them. For example, if you have a "Quiz Series" method, the quiz can be a part of the newsletter.

Step 10 – Archive and Access: Create a digital archive or repository where past newsletters can be accessed. This provides a resource for participants who want to revisit previous themes or for those who missed earlier editions.

FEATURES OF THE TECHNIQUE

Type	Resource
Frequency	Recurring
Timing	Over time after the training
Pacing	Scheduled
Real-Time Trainer Input	No
Participation	Individual
Automation	Partial (for scheduling)
Client Facilitation	No
Live Event	No
Specialist Tools Needed	No

VIDEO REMINDERS – IMPROMPTU

A PERSONALIZED APPROACH TO REINFORCING TRAINING

SEND A SHORT VIDEO TO training participants one month after the program and include a quick reminder of the key points from the training, actions they can take, and encouragement to keep practicing. The videos can include references to events or examples from the main training event to give a more personal touch. These videos serve as both a refresher and a motivational tool, ensuring that the key takeaways from the training remain top-of-mind for participants.

1. **Content Creation:** After the training event, the trainer or facilitator should record a video succinctly recapping the main points and emphasizing the most critical concepts and techniques from the training.
2. **Actionable Steps:** Include actionable steps viewers can take to further implement their learning, which might include exercises, real-world applications of the training, or even challenges to test their knowledge.
3. **Personal Touch:** Video messages allow for a more personalized and engaging experience. Address common questions that arose during the training, share additional resources, or even provide feedback on progress made by the group.

4. **Distribution:** Once the video is recorded, send a link to the video to all training participants via email or through the company's communication platform.

CREATING AND IMPLEMENTING "VIDEO REMINDERS – IMPROMPTU" METHOD

Step 1 – Preparation: Review the main content and objectives of the training session to determine the key points you want to emphasize in the video. Include notable examples, stories, and moments from the main training session.

Step 2 – Plan Your Video: Outline the content of your video. Decide on the sequence of topics, any actionable steps you want to include, and any additional resources or challenges you want to mention. Keep the video concise, aiming for a duration that's engaging but not overwhelming (typically 5-10 minutes).

Step 3 – Record the Video: Find a quiet space with good lighting. Start recording, ensuring you speak clearly and engage directly with the camera to create a personal connection. Use visuals or screen sharing when necessary to emphasize points or show examples. (Tools like Loom are great for this.)

Step 4 – Edit and Review: Once recorded, trim any unnecessary parts. Review the video to ensure clarity, coherence, and that all key points are covered.

Step 5 – Upload and Generate Link: Save and upload your video to a sharable location. Once uploaded, generate a shareable link for distribution.

Step 6 – Distribute the Video: Send the video link to all training participants. This can be done via email, company communication platforms, or any other preferred method. In your message, provide context about the video's purpose and encourage participants to watch it in its entirety.

FEATURES OF THE TECHNIQUE

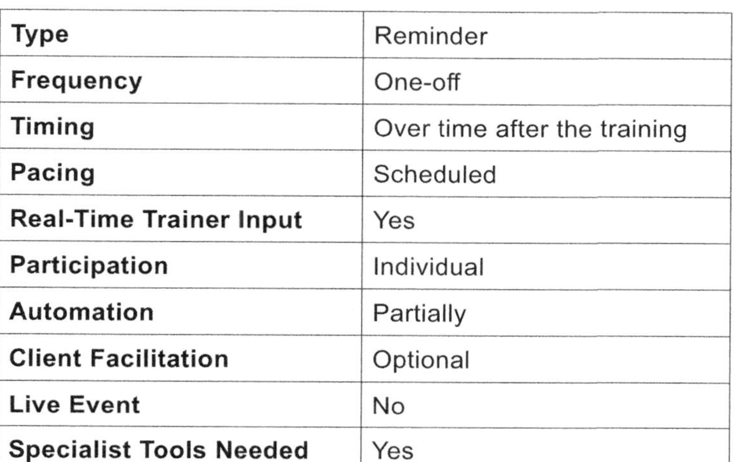

Type	Reminder
Frequency	One-off
Timing	Over time after the training
Pacing	Scheduled
Real-Time Trainer Input	Yes
Participation	Individual
Automation	Partially
Client Facilitation	Optional
Live Event	No
Specialist Tools Needed	Yes

VIDEO REMINDERS – SCHEDULED

A REINFORCEMENT STRATEGY FOR LONG-TERM RETENTION

RECORD ONE- OR TWO-MINUTE VIDEO reminders of key points from the training and send them to trainees throughout the year. Similar to animated videos, these videos should serve as bite-sized refreshers designed to jog the memory of participants and reinforce the training's key takeaways, but they should include you instead of animation. These differ from impromptu video reminders by being pre-recorded and reusable for multiple instances of the same training with different trainees.

1. **Content Identification:** Begin by pinpointing the most crucial elements of the training that would benefit from periodic reminders.
2. **Video Production:** Record succinct videos that clearly and engagingly convey each key point. The emphasis here is on brevity and clarity.
3. **Scheduling:** Distribute these videos at regular intervals throughout the year. This could be monthly, bi-monthly, or even quarterly, depending on the training's complexity and the retention needs of the participants.
4. **Distribution:** Utilize email, company intranets, messaging apps, or Learning Management Systems (LMS) to send out these video reminders. Ensure that the platform used supports easy video playback and is accessible to all participants.

CREATING AND IMPLEMENTING "VIDEO REMINDERS" METHOD

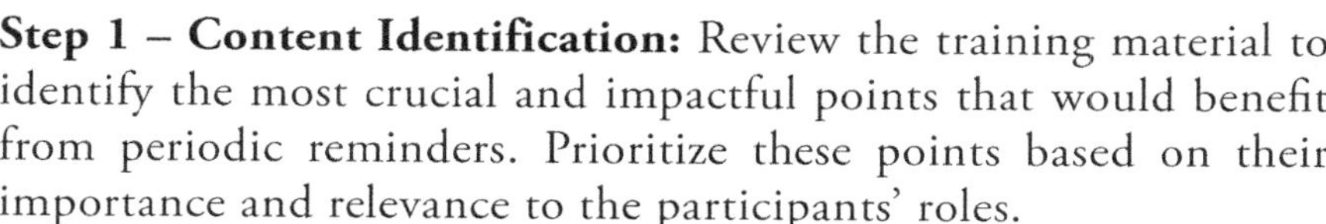

Step 1 – Content Identification: Review the training material to identify the most crucial and impactful points that would benefit from periodic reminders. Prioritize these points based on their importance and relevance to the participants' roles.

Step 2 – Scripting: Write concise scripts for each video. Ensure that each script is clear, engaging, and can be delivered within the one-minute timeframe. Review and refine scripts to eliminate jargon and ensure clarity.

Step 3 – Video Production: Choose a quiet location with good lighting. Use a smartphone, webcam, or professional camera, depending on your budget and desired video quality. Consider using visuals, props, or slides to emphasize key points. Record and then edit the videos for clarity, adding captions or graphics as needed.

Step 4 – Platform Selection: Decide on the platform or medium for distributing the videos. This could be via email, company intranets, messaging apps, or a Learning Management System (LMS). Ensure the chosen platform supports video playback and is accessible to all participants.

Step 5 – Write Messages: Write a message to accompany each video. The message should be appropriately formatted for the delivery platform and could be emails, Slack, MS teams announcements, or some other format. Introduce the video, use intrigue to encourage trainees to view the video. Remind the recipient which training event it relates to.

Step 6 – Scheduling: Plan a distribution schedule for the videos. This could be weekly, bi-weekly, monthly, etc. Use automated tools or reminders to ensure timely distribution.

Step 7 – Distribution: Upload the videos to the chosen platform, sending them out according to the predetermined schedule. Ensure that participants receive notifications when a new video is available.

FEATURES OF THE TECHNIQUE

Type	Reminder
Frequency	Recurring
Timing	Ongoing after the training
Pacing	Scheduled
Real-Time Trainer Input	Yes
Participation	Individual
Automation	Yes
Client Facilitation	Optional
Live Event	No
Specialist Tools Needed	No

EXAMPLE

To see an example of recap videos, look for the series of videos covering the key points from my training program "15 Steps for Successful Meetings" on my YouTube Channel: https://www.youtube.com/@chrisfenningcommunication/playlists

ACTIVITIES

Activities provide a change from the passive receipt of reminders. Trainees have to take action, answer questions, complete tasks, and more. In this section, you'll find a selection of activity-based strategies that help learners engage with the material, test themselves, and transform theory into real-world skills.

These methods require more real-time involvement from you as the trainer compared to the reminders and reinforcement methods, but there is still the opportunity for some automation. The increase in time is offset by the increase in trainee engagement and the improved retention of learning that occurs when people actively apply what they learn.

When choosing an activity-based method to support your training, keep in mind the time involved for both yourself and the trainees. Activities should not feel like a burden to the learners.

11. **Challenges:** Engaging Trainees Through Competitive Learning
12. **Follow-Up Actions – Trainee Defined:** Personal Commitments for Tangible Implementation
13. **Follow-Up Actions – Trainer Defined:** Structured Steps for Immediate Application
14. **Interactive Email Challenges:** Engaging Trainees Beyond the Classroom

15. **Participant-Generated Content:** Empowering Trainees to Become Contributors
16. **Quiz Series:** Gamified Recall and Reinforcement
17. **Storytelling Series:** Harnessing the Power of Narrative
18. **Teach Someone Else:** The Power of Peer-to-Peer Knowledge Transfer

CASE STUDY

In the weeks following the completion of an extensive training for customer complaint handling, the learners from a government department applied what they had learned by completing actions they had defined for themselves during the training.

Initially, the application of methods from the training was good, but after a few weeks, the learners had slipped back into their old habits. Observing a return to the pre-training levels of customer complaints, the training team reconnected with the learners and introduced a series of challenges and quizzes. The good-natured competition saw employees actively engage in competitive learning and apply their skills to win rewards.

But the most transformative method was "Teach Someone Else." Each trainee was tasked with educating a peer, thereby cementing their own understanding through teaching. The results were impressive—not only did knowledge retention improve, leading to a reduction in the number of customer complaints, but the trainees also suggested team prizes and worked to educate new team members to enhance their team knowledge and help them win one of the monthly prizes.

CHALLENGES

ENGAGING TRAINEES THROUGH COMPETITIVE LEARNING

SET UP MONTHLY CHALLENGES WHERE participants have to tackle unique hurdles or puzzles related to the training topic. Challenges introduce an element of competition and peer evaluation into the post-training phase. By setting up monthly challenges related to the training topic, trainees are not only encouraged to apply what they've learned but also to think creatively and critically about real-world applications. These challenges, often presented as puzzles or scenarios, should be shared on an internal platform where peers can evaluate, discuss, and vote on the most effective and innovative solutions.

1. **Challenge Design:** Design a series of challenges related to the training content. These challenges should be practical, relevant, and require trainees to apply their knowledge in innovative ways.
2. **Platform Setup:** Utilize an internal platform or forum where challenges can be posted and trainees can submit their responses. This could be an intranet, a dedicated website, or even a chat application.
3. **Monthly Challenge Release:** At the start of each month, release a new challenge and give trainees a set timeframe (e.g., a week or two) to submit their solutions.

4. **Peer Evaluation:** Once solutions are submitted, trainees should be able to view the responses of their peers and discuss, provide feedback, and ultimately vote on the solutions they find most effective.
5. **Recognition & Reward:** At the end of the voting period, recognize the top solutions (as voted by peers). Consider offering rewards or incentives to motivate participation and excellence.
6. **Feedback Loop:** Trainers should provide feedback on the solutions, highlighting the strengths of top responses and offering insights on areas of improvement.

CREATING AND IMPLEMENTING "THE CHALLENGES" METHOD

Step 1 – Define the Objective: Clearly outline what you aim to achieve with each challenge. This could be reinforcing a specific training concept, encouraging creative application, or fostering collaborative problem-solving.

Step 2 – Choose an Internal Platform: Decide on an appropriate platform where challenges will be posted and trainees can submit responses. This could be an existing company intranet, a dedicated website, or a chat application.

Step 3 – Design the Challenges: Create a series of challenges related to the training content. Ensure they are practical, relevant, and vary in complexity to cater to all skill levels. Wherever possible, incorporate real-world scenarios or problems trainees might encounter in their roles.

Step 4 – Set the Rules: Clearly define the rules for participation. This includes submission guidelines, the timeframe for each challenge, and the voting process. Decide on how feedback will be provided, both from peers and trainers.

Step 5 – Launch the First Challenge: Announce and release the first challenge, ensuring all trainees are informed and have access to the platform. Provide any necessary resources or guidelines to help trainees tackle the challenge.

Step 6 – Monitor Participation: Regularly check the platform to gauge participation levels and ensure discussions remain constructive. Address any technical issues or queries that arise.

Step 7 – Facilitate Peer Evaluation: Once the submission period ends, open the platform for peer evaluation. Trainees can view, discuss, and vote on their peers' solutions. Encourage constructive feedback and productive discussions.

Step 8 – Announce Top Solutions: At the end of the voting period, highlight the top solutions based on peer votes. Consider offering rewards or recognition to those with the most effective or innovative solutions.

Step 9 – Provide Comprehensive Feedback: Trainers should offer feedback on the submitted solutions. Highlight the strengths of top responses and provide insights on areas that can be improved. This feedback can be shared on the platform or during a dedicated review session.

Step 10 – Schedule and Release Subsequent Challenges: Continue releasing new challenges at regular intervals (e.g., monthly) to maintain engagement and reinforce training content.

FEATURES OF THE TECHNIQUE

Type	Activity
Frequency	Recurring
Timing	Over time after the training
Pacing	Scheduled
Real-Time Trainer Input	Yes
Participation	Individual
Automation	Partially
Client Facilitation	Optional
Live Event	Possibly
Specialist Tools Needed	No

EXAMPLE

Here is an example of a challenge structure from a B2B sales training program.

Challenge Series Objective: Reinforce B2B sales techniques, foster creative problem-solving, and encourage collaboration among sales teams.

Platform: A dedicated channel on the company's Slack workspace named #B2B-Sales-Challenges.

Rules:

- Each challenge begins on the first Monday of the month and runs for two weeks.
- Submissions can be in the form of text, video, or audio, depending on the challenge.
- Peer evaluations (likes, comments, and constructive feedback) will take place during the third week of the month.
- Top solutions will be highlighted in the last week of the month and the highest voted submission wins a $25 Amazon gift card and bragging rights.

Challenge Topics (Use One Per Month):

1. **Cold Outreach Techniques:** Challenge participants to craft a compelling cold email to a potential high-value client in a new industry the company is targeting.
2. **Overcoming Objections:** Present a scenario where a potential client has a specific objection to the product/service. Ask participants to come up with a response that addresses the objection while highlighting the product's value.
3. **Product Pitch:** Introduce a new feature of the product/service and challenge participants to create a 2-minute video pitch targeting a specific client segment.
4. **Negotiation Scenarios:** Describe a situation where a potential client is asking for significant discounts or additional perks. Challenge participants to negotiate a deal that maintains profitability while securing the client.

5. **Client Retention:** Present a scenario where a long-term client is considering switching to a competitor. Ask participants to devise a strategy to retain the client.

First Challenge Launch:

Announcement on Slack:

- "Hello team! Excited to kick off our first B2B Sales Challenge. This month, we're focusing on Cold Outreach Techniques. Your task? Craft a compelling cold email to EcoTech Industries, a potential high-value client in the sustainable technology sector. Remember, they've never heard of us before! Submit your emails here by [date]. Looking forward to your innovative approaches!"

Monitoring and Evaluation:

- The sales training team will monitor submissions, ensuring that discussions remain constructive.
- Peer evaluations will be encouraged through likes and comments. Constructive feedback is a must!

Announcement of Top Solutions:

- "Congratulations to [names of top participants] for their outstanding cold outreach emails! Check out their innovative approaches [link to top submissions]. Stay tuned for next month's challenge on Overcoming Objections!"

Feedback Collection:

- At the end of the month, a short survey will be shared. We'd love to hear your thoughts on this month's B2B Sales Challenge. What did you learn? What can we improve? Your feedback will shape future challenges!

Refinement:

- Based on feedback and participation rates, the challenges can be refined. For instance, if participants find video submissions challenging, future challenges can focus more on text-based tasks.

FOLLOW-UP ACTIONS – TRAINEE DEFINED

PERSONAL COMMITMENTS FOR TANGIBLE IMPLEMENTATION

AT THE END OF THE training event, have participants commit to two or three follow-up actions they will take to implement what they have learned. Instead of prescribing a one-size-fits-all post-training action plan, trainees can identify and commit to specific actions that resonate most with their personal learning journey and professional context. By having trainees define their own follow-up actions and holding them accountable to their commitments, the training becomes more personalized, relevant, and actionable.

1. **Reflection Time:** Toward the end of the training session, allocate time for trainees to reflect on what they've learned. This introspective period allows them to sift through the content and identify what resonates most with them.
2. **Guided Action Planning:** Encourage trainees to think about how they can apply their newfound knowledge in their daily roles. Provide guiding questions or prompts to help them consider practical applications. This might include sections like Key Takeaways, Action Steps, Potential Challenges, and Resources Needed.

3. **Commitment to Actions:** Ask each trainee to define two or three specific actions they commit to taking post-training. These actions should be SMARTR (Specific, Measurable, Achievable, Relevant, Time-bound, Realistic) to increase the likelihood of follow-through.
4. **Sharing and Accountability:** Prompt trainees to share their commitments with the group. This public declaration increases accountability and can inspire others to consider similar actions. Participants also work with an accountability buddy or a designated champion within the organization.
5. **Documentation:** Have trainees document their commitments either on paper, digitally, or within a training platform. This serves as a tangible reminder of their post-training goals.
6. **Follow-Up:** Schedule check-ins or reminders after the training to see how trainees are progressing with their self-defined actions. This can be done through emails, meetings, or digital platforms.

CREATING AND IMPLEMENTING "FOLLOW-UP ACTIONS – TRAINEE DEFINED" METHOD

Step 1 – Prepare Guiding Questions: Develop a set of guiding questions or prompts that can help trainees think about practical applications of the training content. These questions should be open-ended and encourage deep thinking.

Step 2 – Communication: During the training session design, clearly communicate the purpose and benefits of defining personal follow-up actions to trainees. This sets the stage for their active participation.

Step 3 – Reflection: Toward the end of the training session, allocate a specific time slot for reflection. This ensures that trainees have a moment to internalize and process the content.

Step 4 – Action Planning: Facilitate a session where trainees identify and document their two or three specific follow-up actions. Use a structure like SMARTR (Specific, Measurable, Achievable,

Relevant, Time-bound, Reviewed) to improve the quality and clarity of the actions. Provide guiding questions or prompts to help them consider practical applications, this might include sections like "Key Takeaways," "Action Steps," "Potential Challenges," and "Resources Needed."

Step 5 – Sharing Mechanism: Create a platform or mechanism where trainees can share their commitments. This could be a physical board in a classroom, a digital platform, or simply sharing aloud in a group setting. Participants also share their actions with an accountability buddy or a designated champion within the organization. This person is responsible for periodically checking in on the participant's progress, offering support, and ensuring that the plan is being followed.

Step 6 – Document Commitments: Ensure that each trainee has a way to document their commitments, whether it's in a training workbook, a digital platform, or via email. This serves as a personal reminder for them.

Step 7 – Schedule Follow-Ups: Set specific dates for follow-up check-ins. These can be individual or group sessions, and they serve to review progress and address any challenges faced in implementing the actions.

Step 8 – Send Reminders: A day or two before the scheduled follow-ups, send reminders to trainees. This can be done via email, SMS, or any other communication platform used by the organization.

Step 9 – Conduct Follow-Up Sessions: During these sessions, allow trainees to discuss their progress, share successes, and address challenges. Celebrate achievements and provide support or guidance for challenges.

Step 10 – Analyze: Document the commitments and outcomes from each training session. Over time, this data can provide insights into the most common actions trainees commit to, their success rates, and areas where additional support might be needed.

FEATURES OF THE TECHNIQUE

Type	Activity
Frequency	One-off
Timing	During the training
Pacing	Self-pace
Real-Time Trainer Input	No
Participation	Individual
Automation	No
Client Facilitation	Optional
Live Event	No
Specialist Tools Needed	No

EXAMPLES

Example 1: Mindfulness

Participants in a mindfulness training wrote these follow-up actions using this slightly modified version of the SMARTR format:

Mindful Breaks

- **Specific**: I will take two 5-minute mindful breaks daily to practice deep breathing and grounding exercises.
- **Measurable**: I'll set alarms on my phone to remind me to take these breaks.
- **Achievable**: I'll keep the exercises simple, using guided sessions from a mindfulness app.
- **Relevant**: Mindfulness has been shown to reduce stress and improve focus.
- **Time-bound**: I'll start this routine tomorrow and continue for the next 30 days.
- **Reviewed**: At the end of the month, I'll assess the impact on my stress levels and decide whether to continue or adjust the practice.

Example 2: Become More Organized

Participants in a "Become More Organized" training wrote these follow-up actions this slightly modified version of the SMARTR format:

Task Prioritization

- **Specific**: I will start each day by listing and prioritizing my tasks.
- **Measurable**: I'll aim to complete at least the top three priority tasks daily.
- **Achievable**: I'll use a digital task manager to organize and prioritize.
- **Relevant**: Prioritizing tasks can reduce feelings of overwhelm and increase productivity.
- **Time-bound**: I'll implement this strategy starting next week and evaluate its effectiveness after two weeks.
- **Reviewed**: After two weeks, I'll review my task completion rate and adjust my approach if necessary.

Tips:

Capture the actions from the trainees so you can use them in future training. The best ones can become part of the Trainer defined follow-up actions method.

How can you capture the actions?

- Ask the trainees to send them to you after the training.
- Photograph / photocopy their actions (or ask them to take a photo and send it to you).

FOLLOW-UP ACTIONS – TRAINER DEFINED

STRUCTURED STEPS FOR IMMEDIATE APPLICATION

At the end of the presentation, give the trainees actions they can take in 10-15 minutes that day, 20 minutes the next, and actions to take over the next week. This differs from the trainee defined actions by providing them with a clear, structured path of actionable steps instead of leaving trainees to work out the next steps on their own. By prescribing specific tasks with varying durations, and a set of actions for the subsequent week, trainees have a tangible roadmap to apply and reinforce their learning.

1. **Action Design:** Based on the training content, design a series of actionable steps that trainees can undertake. These actions should include a mix of quick tasks to more involved ones.
2. **Immediate Application:** Right after the training, give trainees tasks they can complete in 10-15 minutes. This immediate application serves to reinforce key training points while they're still fresh.
3. **Next Day Reinforcement:** The following day, have trainees delve deeper with a 20-minute task. This reinforces the previous day's learning and introduces new facets or applications of the training content.

4. **Extended Application:** Over the subsequent weeks, give trainees a series of actions that allow them to explore the training content in more depth, apply it in various contexts, and integrate it into their regular routines.

CREATING AND IMPLEMENTING "FOLLOW-UP ACTIONS – TRAINER DEFINED" METHOD

Step 1 – Content Review: Identify key concepts, skills, or knowledge areas that would benefit from immediate and extended application.

Step 2 – Design Immediate Actions: Craft specific tasks that trainees can complete in 10-15 minutes immediately after the training. These should be simple, relevant, and directly tied to the core training content.

Step 3 – Design Next Day Actions: Develop a slightly more involved task or set of tasks that trainees can undertake the following day, requiring about 20 minutes. This should build on the immediate actions and delve deeper into the training content.

Step 4 – Design Extended Actions: Outline a series of actions for trainees to take over the subsequent weeks. These can range from practical applications and exercises to reflections and further readings. Tasks can be quick (5-10 minutes) or more involved (30-60 minutes).

Step 5 – Create Clear Instructions: For each action, provide clear, concise instructions. If necessary, include resources, templates, or tools that trainees might need to complete the tasks.

Step 6 – Integrate into Training Session: Toward the end of the training session, introduce the concept of the follow-up actions. Clearly explain the purpose, benefits, and the structure of the tasks they'll be undertaking.

Step 7 – Distribute Action Plans: Hand out the action plans to trainees, either in printed form, digitally, or via a training platform. Ensure each trainee has easy access to their set of tasks.

Step 8 – Encourage Commitment: Ask trainees to verbally or mentally commit to completing the tasks. This can enhance their sense of accountability and increase the likelihood of follow-through.

Step 9 – Set Up Feedback Channels: Establish channels where trainees can share their experiences, ask questions, or seek feedback as they work through their tasks. This could be a digital forum, group chats, or scheduled check-in sessions.

Step 10 – Monitor Progress: Track trainee progress through the tasks. This can be done through self-reporting, digital platforms, or during feedback sessions.

FEATURES OF THE TECHNIQUE

Type	Activity
Frequency	One-off
Timing	During the training
Pacing	Self-pace
Real-Time Trainer Input	No
Participation	Individual
Automation	No
Client Facilitation	Optional
Live Event	No
Specialist Tools Needed	No

INTERACTIVE EMAIL CHALLENGES

ENGAGING TRAINEES BEYOND THE CLASSROOM

SEND OUT WEEKLY OR MONTHLY email challenges where participants have to respond to a hypothetical scenario relevant to their work. Trainees reply directly to the email, and the best responses could be shared (with permission) in the next email. The challenges help trainees to apply their knowledge in scenarios relevant to their work. Adding a feedback and review process adds an element of competitiveness and group interaction to the process.

1. **Content Creation:** Design hypothetical scenarios that are relevant to the training topic and the work or role of the trainees. These scenarios should be realistic, thought-provoking, and require the application of the concepts taught during the training.
2. **Email Distribution:** Send out these scenarios as weekly challenges to the participants. The message should be well-designed, concise, and clearly state the challenge. It should also provide instructions on how to respond and a deadline for submissions.
3. **Participant Interaction:** Have trainees respond directly to the email, detailing how they would handle the presented scenario based on their training.
4. **Review and Selection:** Once the deadline is reached, the training team reviews the responses. They can select the most insightful, innovative, or effective solutions.

5. **Feedback and Sharing:** In the subsequent challenge email, with the participant's permission, share the best responses from the previous challenge. This not only recognizes and celebrates the trainee's efforts but also provides diverse perspectives and solutions to the entire group.
6. **Periodic Summaries:** Every few months, send out a summary email highlighting the most notable solutions, key learning points, and any patterns or common misconceptions observed in the responses.

NOTE: *This method differs from the other "Challenges" method because this is not a group activity. Trainees reply to the trainer directly via email, and there is no formal voting or discussion with other trainees.*

CREATING AND IMPLEMENTING "INTERACTIVE EMAIL CHALLENGES" METHOD

Step 1 – Define Objectives: Clearly outline what you aim to achieve with the email challenges. This could range from reinforcing specific training concepts to fostering collaborative learning among participants.

Step 2 – Scenario Development: Design a series of hypothetical scenarios relevant to the training topic and to the work the trainees do. Ensure they are realistic, engaging, and require the application of the training's key concepts.

Step 3 – Email Template Design: Create a visually appealing and easy-to-read email template. The design should include space for the challenge, instructions on how to respond, and a section for sharing previous challenge responses. Make sure the content meets accessibility and DEI standards.

Step 4 – Set Up a Mailing List (Optional): Compile a list of all training participants' email addresses. If you are an independent trainer, consider using email distribution platforms like Mailchimp or Constant Contact to manage and automate the email challenges.

Step 5 – Schedule the Emails: Decide on the frequency (e.g., weekly or monthly) and set specific dates for sending out the challenges. If using an email platform, you can schedule these in advance.

Step 6 – Send the First Challenge: Send the first email challenge to the participants. Ensure it includes clear instructions on how to respond and the deadline for submissions.

Step 7 – Review Responses: After the deadline, review all the responses received. Evaluate them based on their alignment with the training concepts, creativity, and practicality.

Step 8 – Select Top Responses: Choose one or more of the best responses to be highlighted in the next email. Ensure you obtain permission from the participants before sharing their answers.

Step 9 – Send the Next Challenge: In the subsequent email, include the top responses from the previous challenge, then present the new challenge. This cycle continues for the duration of your email challenge campaign.

Step 10 – Periodic Summaries: Every few months, send a summary email highlighting key insights, notable solutions, and patterns observed from the challenges. This serves as a recap and reinforces the learning.

FEATURES OF THE TECHNIQUE

Type	Activity
Frequency	Recurring
Timing	Ongoing after the training
Pacing	Scheduled
Real-Time Trainer Input	Yes
Participation	Individuals
Automation	Partial
Client Facilitation	Optional
Live Event	No
Specialist Tools Needed	No

EXAMPLE

Here is an example of a challenge email from training about intermediate level Excel skills. This challenge is intended to test the trainees use of specific functions they learned in the training (VLOOKUP, IFERROR, Remove Duplicates, Pivot Tables, Charts)

Subject: Weekly Challenge: Can you pivot this data?

Hello [Participant's Name],

As part of our ongoing training on intermediate Excel skills, we're excited to bring you this week's interactive email challenge. Remember, the goal is to apply the skills you've learned and to challenge yourself in real-world scenarios.

Here's what to do:

- **Step 1:** Read the scenario information.
- **Step 2:** Complete the task described in the Challenge section.
- **Step 3:** Email your response.

<u>The Challenge: Can you pivot this data?</u>

Scenario: You've been given an Excel file of data from the sales team. Apparently, it contains all the sales information from every sales person from the previous three years. You've been asked to review, tidy, and analyze the data, then present a summary of what's included to your manager.

Your challenge is:

1. Remove duplicates.
2. Find and highlight any missing data.
3. Create a summary of the sales performance in each year.
4. Compare each year against the previous year.

Output: You can provide the summary in any format that effectively communicates your findings.

Please reply directly to this email with your summary by *[specific deadline, e.g., Friday, 5 PM]*.

We're eager to see your responses! The best summaries will be shared in our next email (with permission, of course). This is a great opportunity to refine your summarization skills and learn from your peers.

Keep up the great work and happy summarizing!

Warm regards,

[Your Name] Training Coordinator

PARTICIPANT-GENERATED CONTENT

EMPOWERING TRAINEES TO BECOME CONTRIBUTORS

ENCOURAGE PARTICIPANTS TO CREATE AND share their own tips, videos, or writings about their journey post-training. This not only serves as a reminder for them but also as content for others. The content they create improves the collective knowledge and insights of the group.

1. **Content Creation Encouragement:** Post-training, encourage participants to create their own content. This could be in the form of short videos, written reflections, infographics, or even audio recordings detailing their experiences, challenges, and successes.
2. **Sharing Platforms:** Organizations can set up platforms where this content can be shared. This could be an internal company blog, a dedicated section on the company intranet, a shared drive, or even a private group on social media platforms.
3. **Moderation and Quality Control:** While it's essential to encourage freedom of expression, there should be a basic moderation process in place to ensure the shared content is appropriate and aligns with company values.

4. **Feedback and Interaction:** Other participants can view, comment on, and learn from the shared content. This interactive element not only reinforces learning but also fosters a sense of community and collaborative growth.
5. **Recognition & Rewards:** To motivate participants to contribute, organizations can introduce recognition systems. For instance, the "Best Tip of the Month" could be highlighted, or contributors could earn badges or other incentives.

CREATING AND IMPLEMENTING "PARTICIPANT-GENERATED CONTENT" METHOD

Step 1 – Set Clear Objectives: Define the purpose of participant-generated content. Is it for reflection, sharing best practices, or showcasing success stories? Determine the desired outcomes, such as increased engagement, deeper understanding, or community building.

Step 2 – Choose Suitable Platforms: Decide where participants will share their content. This could be an internal portal, a company blog, a dedicated social media group, or a shared drive. Ensure the platform is accessible to all participants and allows for easy content uploading and commenting.

Step 3 – Provide Guidelines: Offer clear guidelines on the type of content participants can create (videos, articles, infographics, etc.). Outline any content length restrictions, preferred formats, and topics to avoid. Share best practices for content creation, such as keeping videos concise or recording audio in a quiet location.

Step 4 – Offer Tools and Resources: Provide participants with tools or resources that can help them with content creation. This might include video recording apps, writing templates, or graphic design tools. Consider hosting a brief workshop on content creation basics to equip participants with essential skills.

Step 5 – Set Up a Moderation System: Designate a team or individual responsible for reviewing and approving submitted content to ensure it aligns with company values and guidelines. Decide on a turnaround time for content review and communicate this to participants.

Step 6 – Foster Engagement: Encourage participants to not only create but also engage with others' content. This can be through commenting, sharing, or providing feedback. Create a system where the most engaging or helpful content is highlighted or rewarded.

Step 7 – Implement Recognition & Rewards: Introduce a system to recognize and reward top contributors. This could be monthly highlights, badges, or even tangible rewards. Publicly acknowledge and appreciate participants who consistently contribute valuable content.

Step 8 – Promote Continuously: Regularly remind participants of the opportunity to share and learn from peer-generated content. Share success stories or impactful content in broader company meetings or communications to showcase the value of the initiative.

Step 9 – Archive and Reuse: Over time, create an organized archive of participant-generated content. This can serve as a valuable resource for future trainees or for refining training materials. Consider repurposing standout content for other company initiatives or training programs.

FEATURES OF THE TECHNIQUE

Type	Activity
Frequency	Recurring
Timing	Over time after the training
Pacing	Self-pace
Real-Time Trainer Input	No (or optional)
Participation	Individual & Group
Automation	No
Client Facilitation	Yes
Live Event	No
Specialist Tools Needed	Content sharing platform

QUIZ SERIES

GAMIFIED RECALL AND REINFORCEMENT

PRESENT TRAINEES WITH A SERIES of quizzes over a set duration to test their recall of the training content and encourage its application in real-world scenarios. The added element of gamification through leaderboards and rewards can inject a competitive spirit, making the learning process more engaging and motivating.

1. **Structured Quiz Deployment:** After the main training event, schedule a series of quizzes to be sent out at predetermined intervals. This could be daily, weekly, or monthly, depending on the training's depth and complexity.
2. **Diverse Question Formats:** The quizzes should incorporate a mix of multiple-choice questions, true/false statements, short answers, and scenario-based questions. This variety ensures a comprehensive assessment of both theoretical knowledge and practical application.
3. **Gamification Elements:**

    - **Leaderboards:** Display top-performing participants based on their quiz scores. This encourages friendly competition and motivates trainees to review and prepare.

- **Rewards:** Offer tangible or intangible rewards for top performers. This could range from certificates and badges to gift vouchers or additional learning opportunities.

4. **Feedback Mechanism:** After each quiz, provide participants with immediate feedback on their performance. Highlight the correct answers and offer brief explanations or references to the training material, reinforcing the learning.

5. **Progress Tracking:** Allow participants to track their progress over time, helping them identify areas of strength and those that might require further review.

CREATING AND IMPLEMENTING "QUIZ SERIES" METHOD

Step 1 – Content Review: Review the training material to identify key concepts, techniques, and principles that should be reinforced through the quizzes.

Step 2 – Quiz Design: Create a series of quizzes with diverse question formats: multiple-choice, true/false, short answers, and scenario-based questions. Ensure questions range from basic recall to application-based to test both memory and understanding.

Step 3 – Choose a Quiz Tool: Automated quiz tools will make setting up and managing the quizzes easier. Many learning course platforms include quiz functions, and there are online tools specifically designed for quizzes. Choose something that all participants can access and fits with the style of your training and the client.

Step 4 – Gamification Setup:

- **Leaderboard.** Design a system to track and display scores. Consider using a platform or tool that supports leaderboards. (e.g., keepthescore.com)
- **Rewards.** Decide on the rewards for top performers. This could be certificates, badges, gift vouchers, or other incentives. Ensure there is budget to cover the costs if applicable.

Step 5 – Schedule Deployment: Determine the frequency of the quizzes (e.g., daily, weekly, monthly). Use an automated system or Learning Management System (LMS) to deploy quizzes at the set intervals.

Step 6 – Communication: Inform participants about the quiz series during the training, explaining its purpose and the added gamification elements. Highlight the benefits, such as reinforcing learning and the potential to earn rewards.

Step 7 – Monitor Participation: Track participation rates. If they're lower than expected, consider sending reminders or additional incentives to boost engagement.

Step 8 – Progress Tracking: Allow participants to view their progress over time. This can be through a dashboard or periodic reports.

Step 9 – Celebrate and Reward: Publicly recognize top performers, whether through company newsletters, meetings, or on the platform itself. Distribute rewards as promised, ensuring transparency in the process.

FEATURES OF THE TECHNIQUE

Type	Activity
Frequency	Recurring
Timing	Over time after the training
Pacing	Scheduled
Real-Time Trainer Input	No
Participation	Individual
Automation	Yes
Client Facilitation	Optional
Live Event	No
Specialist Tools Needed	Quiz tool and leaderboard

EXAMPLE

Here are some example quiz questions from a 1-day digital photography for beginners course. The trainer sent an email to the course participants with a short message and a link to an online quiz platform where they can view the questions and submit their answers.

Multiple-Choice Questions

1. Which of the following is NOT a primary setting on the exposure triangle?

    a) ISO

    b) Shutter Speed

    c) Aperture

    d) White Balance

2. What does a fast shutter speed do?

    a) Blurs motion

    b) Freezes motion

    c) Increases light exposure

    d) Decreases depth of field

True/False Statements

3. **True or False:** A larger aperture (like f/1.8) will give a shallower depth of field compared to a smaller aperture (like f/16).
4. **True or False:** A lower ISO setting will result in more noise in the image.

Short Answer Question

5. What is the rule of thirds in photography?

Scenario-Based Questions

6. You're photographing a sports event indoors with dim lighting. You want to freeze the action without introducing a lot of noise. Which of the following settings would be most appropriate?

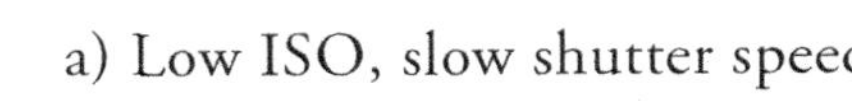

   a) Low ISO, slow shutter speed

   b) High ISO, slow shutter speed

   c) Low ISO, fast shutter speed

   d) High ISO, fast shutter speed

7. You're taking a portrait of a person with a beautiful mountain range in the background. You want both the person and the mountains to be in focus. Which aperture setting would be most suitable?

   a) f/1.8

   b) f/5.6

   c) f/11

   d) f/22

STORYTELLING SERIES

HARNESSING THE POWER OF NARRATIVE

After the training, encourage participants to share real-life instances where they've successfully applied their newfound knowledge or skills. Send out these stories as inspiring examples for others. This taps into the human fondness for stories, creates a shared learning experience, and a sense of community. By transforming abstract concepts into tangible, relatable narratives, this method offers a compelling way to reinforce and revisit training content.

1. **Gather Stories:** After the training, have participants document and share real-life instances where they've applied their newfound knowledge or skills. This could be in written form, through video testimonials, or even audio recordings.
2. **Curation and Editing:** Once stories are collected, select and organize based on clarity, relevance, and impact that aligns with your messaging and training outline. They might be edited to ensure they're concise and effectively convey the key message.
3. **Distribution:** Share these stories among the participants and possibly wider to the organization. This could be done through newsletters, internal communication platforms, or even during team meetings.

4. **Feedback Loop:** After each story is shared, encourage recipients to provide feedback, share their own experiences, or discuss the lessons highlighted in the story.
5. **Recognition:** Recognize and convey appreciation to the individuals who share their stories, further motivating others to contribute to the series.

CREATING AND IMPLEMENTING "STORYTELLING SERIES" METHOD

Step 1 – Set Clear Objectives: Determine what you aim to achieve with the storytelling series. This could be reinforcing key training concepts, promoting a culture of continuous learning, or fostering community among participants.

Step 2 – Create a Submission Platform: Set up a dedicated platform or channel where participants can submit their stories. This could be an email address, an internal portal, or even a shared document.

Step 3 – Communication: During the training, announce the initiative to all training participants. Explain the purpose, the process, and the benefits of sharing and listening to stories.

Step 4 – Provide Guidelines: Offer participants a structure or template for their stories to ensure consistency. This might include a brief introduction, the challenge faced, how training was applied, and the outcome.

Step 5 – Set a Deadline: Give participants a timeframe within which they should submit their stories. This creates a sense of urgency and commitment.

Step 6 – Curate and Edit: Once stories are received, review them for clarity and relevance. Edit as necessary, ensuring the essence of the story remains intact.

Step 7 – Schedule Releases: Plan a schedule for releasing the stories. This could be weekly, bi-weekly, or monthly, depending on the volume of submissions and the duration of the initiative.

Step 8 – Distribute the Stories: Share the curated stories through the chosen medium, be it newsletters, internal communication platforms, or team meetings.

Step 9 – Encourage Feedback: After each story is shared, invite feedback and discussions. This can be done through comments, forums, or even dedicated discussion sessions.

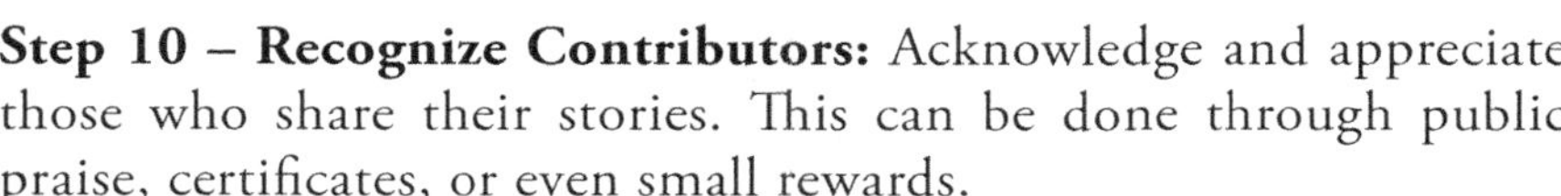

Step 10 – Recognize Contributors: Acknowledge and appreciate those who share their stories. This can be done through public praise, certificates, or even small rewards.

Step 11 – Periodic Reminders: Send out reminders encouraging more participants to share their stories, especially if submissions dwindle over time.

Step 12 – Archive and Access: Create an archive or repository of all shared stories. This ensures that even new employees or those who missed earlier stories can access and benefit from them.

FEATURES OF THE TECHNIQUE

Type	Activity
Frequency	Recurring
Timing	Over time after the training
Pacing	Scheduled
Real-Time Trainer Input	Yes
Participation	Individual
Automation	No
Client Facilitation	Yes
Live Event	No
Specialist Tools Needed	No

TEACH SOMEONE ELSE

THE POWER OF PEER-TO-PEER KNOWLEDGE TRANSFER

ONE OF THE MOST EFFECTIVE ways to learn a topic is to teach it to someone else. This also tests how much the participants have learned. Participants should pick something from the training that they will teach to someone else in the next 48 hours. By encouraging participants to relay their newly acquired knowledge to another individual, they not only reinforce their own understanding but also spread the knowledge further within the organization or community.

1. **Selection of Topic:** At the conclusion of the training session, prompt participants to select a specific topic or skill they found particularly valuable or intriguing.
2. **Commitment to Teach:** Ask participants to commit to teaching this chosen topic to someone else. Make this commitment tangible by having them write down both the topic and the name of the person they intend to teach.
3. **Timeframe:** Set a specific timeframe, typically 48 hours, to ensure immediacy and to capitalize on the fresh memory of the training content.

CREATING AND IMPLEMENTING "TEACH SOMEONE ELSE" METHOD

Step 1 – Introduce the Concept: At the beginning of the training, inform the participants they will be asked to teach a chosen topic to someone else after the session. This sets the expectation and primes them to be on the lookout for key takeaways.

Step 2 – Facilitate Topic Selection: Toward the end of the training, remind participants of the teaching task. Ask them to reflect on the session and identify one key concept, skill, or topic they found particularly valuable.

Step 3 – Commitment Card: Distribute cards or digital forms where participants can write down the topic they've chosen and the name of the person they commit to teaching.

Step 4 – Set a Timeframe: Emphasize the importance of teaching the topic within the next 48 hours. This ensures the material is still fresh in their minds and increases the likelihood of follow-through.

Step 5 – Provide Support Materials: Offer participants supplementary materials, like handouts, slides, or digital resources, to help them in their teaching task.

Step 6 – Encourage Documentation: Ask participants to jot down or digitally record their teaching experience, noting any challenges, questions, or insights that arose during the process.

Step 7 – Follow-Up: After the 48-hour window, send out a reminder email or notification asking participants to share their experiences. This can be done through a survey, a digital platform, or during a follow-up session.

Step 8 – Share Experiences: Organize a debriefing session where participants can voluntarily share their teaching experiences, discuss challenges, and celebrate successes. This can be done in-person or through a digital platform.

FEATURES OF THE TECHNIQUE

Type	Activity
Frequency	One-off
Timing	During and after the training
Pacing	Self-pace within a limited time frame
Real-Time Trainer Input	No
Participation	Individual
Automation	No
Client Facilitation	Optional
Live Event	No
Specialist Tools Needed	No

RECOGNITION & REWARD

When trainees feel acknowledged for their application of new skills, it not only reinforces their learning but also boosts morale and motivates continued professional development. As you explore the methods in this section, think of them not merely as rewards but as strategic investments in your trainees' growth and your organization's future. These methods are about engraining a culture of learning, recognition, and advancement for both individuals and the company.

If budget is an issue, remember that rewards don't have to be financial. Ask the teams to suggest rewards that are non-financial, and you'll likely be surprised by what they come up with. Access to a coveted parking spot for a week or leaving early on a Friday are just a couple of ways to reward people.

If you want to reward trainees for the application of what they learned, try these methods.

19. **Digital Badges & Certifications:** Recognizing and Rewarding Skill Application
20. **Digital Stickers:** Fun and Engaging Training Reminders
21. **Recognition & Reward:** Celebrating Application and Mastery

CASE STUDY

After introducing new software at a graphic design firm, post-training engagement with the tool was faltering until they introduced a system of Digital Badges & Certifications. But the company didn't stop there. They also started a Recognition & Reward system that celebrated the application of skills in real-world projects. Employees voted, and those who exemplified the training principles in their work were publicly acknowledged, creating role models and setting a benchmark for excellence.

Suddenly, trainees had a visual and tangible representation of their progress. These digital accolades became coveted items, symbolizing the recognition of their growing expertise. They served to embed the new software into daily activities and ensured the value of the training investment wasn't lost.

DIGITAL BADGES & CERTIFICATIONS

RECOGNIZING AND REWARDING SKILL APPLICATION

Create a system of digital badges and/or certifications participants can earn when they showcase the use of specific techniques they have learned. They can display these badges on their internal company profiles, email signatures, or LinkedIn profiles. Digital badges and certifications are much like traditional certificates or accolades in that they serve as a visual representation of competencies gained. However, their digital nature allows for broader visibility in an online-centric professional landscape. By earning and displaying these awards, trainees not only gain a sense of accomplishment but also showcase their commitment to continuous learning and professional growth.

1. **Badge Design and Categorization:** Identify specific skills or techniques you feel are worthy of recognition. For each one, design a unique digital badge or certificate. These can range from basic (indicating foundational knowledge) to advanced (indicating mastery).
2. **Criteria Setting:** Clearly define the criteria for earning each badge. This could be based on practical application, passing a test, or showcasing the use of a specific technique in a real-world scenario.

3. **Delivery Platforms:** Use platforms or tools that support the validation and awarding of digital badges. These platforms allow trainers to issue badges, and recipients can then display them on various online platforms.
4. **Earning the Badge:** Trainees can showcase their skills, either as individuals or collectively in a team. Skills are demonstrated through practical application, tests, or demonstrations. Upon successful validation, they earn the respective badge.
5. **Badge Display:** Once earned, trainees can integrate these badges into their internal company profiles, email signatures, LinkedIn profiles, or even personal websites. Some advanced platforms also allow for verification so anyone viewing the badge can confirm its authenticity.
6. **Periodic Renewal:** For certain skills that might evolve over time, consider having badges that require periodic renewal, ensuring trainees keep their knowledge up-to-date.

CREATING AND IMPLEMENTING "DIGITAL BADGES & CERTIFICATIONS" METHOD

Step 1 – Identify Key Skills and Competencies: Review the training content and identify distinct skills, techniques, or knowledge areas that can be recognized with badges or certifications.

Step 2 – Design the Badges and/or Certificates (Outsourcing Optional): Collaborate with a graphic designer to create visually appealing and distinct badges/certificate for each skill or competency. Ensure each badge visually represents its corresponding skill or skill level.

Step 3 – Define Criteria for Earning Badges and Certificates: Clearly outline the requirements or tasks trainees must complete to earn each badge. This could involve practical demonstrations, tests, or real-world application of skills as observed by others. Some badges and certificates may be earned by groups of people working together to demonstrate a particular skill.

Step 4 – Choose a Digital Platform: Select a platform that supports digital badging or certificate delivery, use a paid option such as Credly, Badgr, or a free service like Mozilla Open Badges. Ensure the platform allows for easy issuing, tracking, and verification of badges and certificates.

Step 5 – Integrate with Learning Management System (LMS) (Optional): If possible, integrate the badging platform with the LMS or training portal*. This allows for seamless tracking of trainee progress and automatic badge issuance upon criteria fulfillment. **The LMS may be your own if you are an independent trainer, or it may be the LMS or training portal in the company the trainees are from.*

Step 6 – Communicate the Badge and/or Certificate System: Inform trainees about the new badge system, explaining its purpose, benefits, and how they can earn and display the badges and certificates they earn.

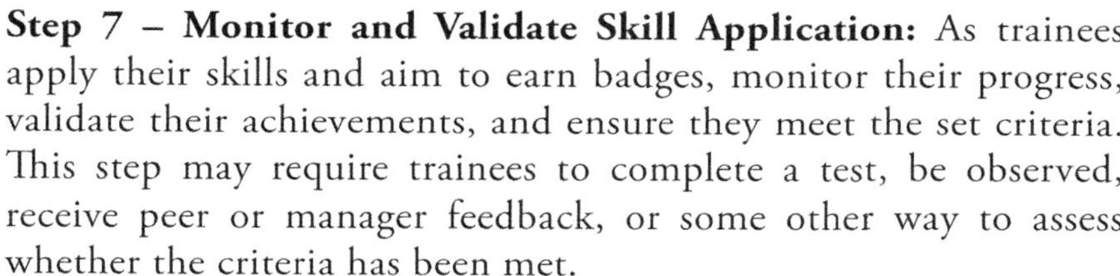

Step 7 – Monitor and Validate Skill Application: As trainees apply their skills and aim to earn badges, monitor their progress, validate their achievements, and ensure they meet the set criteria. This step may require trainees to complete a test, be observed, receive peer or manager feedback, or some other way to assess whether the criteria has been met.

Step 8 – Issue Badges and/or Certificates: Once trainees fulfill the criteria, issue the corresponding badges and/or certificates through the chosen platform. Provide trainees with instructions on how to display their awards on internal company profiles, email signatures, LinkedIn profiles, or personal websites.

Step 9 – Encourage Peer Sharing: Foster a culture where trainees are encouraged to share their achievements with peers, sparking discussions and peer learning.

Step 10 – Periodic Review and Renewal: For skills that evolve over time, set expiration dates on badges and certificates and inform trainees about renewal processes, ensuring their knowledge remains current.

FEATURES OF THE TECHNIQUE

Type	Other
Frequency	Recurring
Timing	Over time after the training
Pacing	Self-pace
Real-Time Trainer Input	No
Participation	Individual or groups
Automation	Yes
Client Facilitation	Yes
Live Event	No
Specialist Tools Needed	Possibly

EXAMPLE

DIGITAL STICKERS

FUN AND ENGAGING TRAINING REMINDERS

Digital Stickers are icons or images that relate to the training and can be shared on various digital communication platforms like Slack, Teams, or Telegram. These stickers should encapsulate key training concepts, techniques, or inside jokes from the training session. Whether they're humorous, motivational, or straightforward, these stickers serve as bite-sized reminders of the training content, seamlessly integrating learning into everyday communication.

1. **Designing the Stickers:** Work with graphic designers to create a series of digital stickers that represent key training concepts. The designs can range from humorous caricatures and memes to straightforward icons or even quotes.
2. **Integration with Platforms:** Once the stickers are designed, they need to be integrated into the desired communication platforms. Each platform will have its own method for adding custom stickers, so follow the respective guidelines.
3. **Promotion and Distribution:** Inform trainees about the availability of these stickers, explaining their purpose and how they can access and use them in their daily communications.
4. **Encourage Usage:** Motivate trainees to use these stickers in relevant contexts. For instance, if a team member applies a training concept successfully in a project, others can acknowledge it by sending the corresponding sticker.

CREATING AND IMPLEMENTING "DIGITAL STICKERS" METHOD

Step 1 – Identify Key Training Concepts: Review the training content to pinpoint essential concepts, techniques, or memorable moments that can be translated into sticker designs.

Step 2 – Design Stickers (Outsourcing Optional): Work with graphic designers or create your own visually appealing stickers. Ensure the designs encapsulate the essence of the training concepts and are suitable for the digital platforms you intend to use.

Step 3 – Choose Suitable Platforms: Decide on which communication platforms (e.g., Slack, Teams, Telegram) the stickers will be used. This decision might be based on the platforms your organization or trainees frequently use.

Step 4 – Format the Stickers: Ensure stickers are in the correct format and size for each platform. Each platform will have its own specifications for custom stickers.

Step 5 – Upload and Integrate: Follow the guidelines of each chosen platform to upload and integrate the custom stickers. This might involve creating a sticker pack or using specific tools or plugins. If working with a client company, you may need to have them implement the stickers in their communication tools.

Step 6 – Announce and Distribute: During the training, tell trainees about the sticker pack. Provide them with instructions on how to access and use the stickers within their communication platforms.

Step 7 – Promote Peer-to-Peer Recognition: Encourage team members to acknowledge each other's application of training concepts by sending the corresponding sticker. This fosters a sense of community and mutual reinforcement.

FEATURES OF THE TECHNIQUE

Type	Other
Frequency	Ongoing
Timing	Immediately after the training
Pacing	Self-pace
Real-Time Trainer Input	No
Participation	Individual
Automation	Yes
Client Facilitation	Yes
Live Event	No
Specialist Tools Needed	Possibly

RECOGNITION & REWARD

CELEBRATING APPLICATION AND MASTERY

RECOGNIZE AND REWARD TRAINEES WHO effectively apply the training in their work through awards, public praise, or other incentives. This motivational approach emphasizes celebrating and acknowledging participants who successfully apply the skills and knowledge they've acquired from training sessions in their day-to-day roles. By offering tangible or intangible rewards, this method reinforces positive behavior and encourages the consistent application of learned techniques.

1. **Criteria Setting:** Before implementing the method, clearly define the criteria for recognition. What specific behaviors or outcomes, indicative of successful training application, will be rewarded?
2. **Monitoring:** Supervisors, team leads, or designated evaluators should monitor and assess employees' application of the training content in their roles.
3. **Nomination:** Employees can be nominated by their peers, supervisors, or even self-nominate, showcasing instances where they've effectively applied their training.
4. **Evaluation:** A committee or designated authority should evaluate the nominations against the set criteria.

5. **Recognition:** Successful nominees are recognized in various ways. This could be through a certificate of achievement, a mention in the company newsletter, or a spotlight in team meetings.
6. **Reward:** Alongside recognition, tangible rewards should be provided. This could range from monetary bonuses, gift cards, additional leave days, to opportunities for further training or career advancement.
7. **Feedback Loop:** Those recognized should be encouraged to share their experiences, tips, and insights with their peers, creating a positive feedback loop and encouraging others to apply their training similarly.

CREATING AND IMPLEMENTING "RECOGNITION & REWARD" METHOD

Step 1 – Define Objectives: Clearly outline what you aim to achieve with the recognition and reward system. This could be increased application of training, improved performance, or fostering a culture of continuous learning.

Step 2 – Set Clear Criteria: Determine the specific behaviors, outcomes, or benchmarks that will qualify for recognition and rewards. Ensure these criteria align with the training's objectives.

Step 3 – Choose When and Where to Deliver Recognition: Decide where and how you'll recognize employees. This could be in team meetings, company newsletters, on an internal digital platform, or during annual award ceremonies.

Step 4 – Determine Rewards: Decide on the types of rewards. These could be monetary (bonuses, gift cards), experiential (extra vacation days, lunch with the CEO), or growth-oriented (courses, books, conference tickets).

Step 5 – Budget Allocation: Ensure there's a dedicated budget for the rewards, especially if they're monetary or experiential. This ensures the sustainability of the program.

Step 6 – Communicate the Initiative: Announce the recognition and reward program to all participants. Clearly communicate the criteria, the process, and the potential rewards.

Step 7 – Monitor and Track: Use performance metrics, feedback tools, or direct observations to monitor how employees are applying their training.

Step 8 – Nomination Process: Allow for peers, supervisors, or individuals to nominate someone (or themselves) for recognition. Ensure there's a simple process in place, like a digital form or a dedicated email address.

Step 9 – Evaluation: Set up a committee or designate individuals to evaluate the nominations against the set criteria. This ensures fairness and consistency in the process.

Step 10 – Announce and Reward: Publicly recognize the individuals who meet or exceed the criteria. Provide them with their rewards promptly to maintain enthusiasm and trust in the system. This can be in team meetings, quarterly newsletters, etc.

Step 11 – Showcase Success Stories: Periodically share stories of those who've been recognized, detailing how they applied their training effectively. This serves as inspiration for others.

Step 12 – Expand or Pivot: If the program is highly successful, consider expanding it to recognize other positive behaviors or achievements. If it's not meeting objectives, consider pivoting to a different method or tweaking the existing one.

FEATURES OF THE TECHNIQUE

Type	Feedback
Frequency	Recurring
Timing	Over time after the training
Pacing	Scheduled
Real-Time Trainer Input	No
Participation	Individual
Automation	No
Client Facilitation	Yes
Live Event	No
Specialist Tools Needed	No

LIVE EVENTS

In this section, we focus on using live interaction to breathe life into post-training support, transforming it from a solo endeavor into a collective journey. Live events provide opportunities to share, learn, and reinforce the training. They not only provide information but also community, collaboration, and real-time support.

These methods require support and/or facilitation from a trainer or someone familiar with the training. As you implement the methods outlined in this section, consider them as your strategy to remind trainees of what they've learned and to inspire them to integrate these learnings with the support of their peers.

To add some human interaction to your training support, try these methods.

22. **Follow-Up Sessions:** Reinforcing Learning Through Scheduled Revisits
23. **Ongoing Support:** Continuous Learning Through Immediate Assistance
24. **Virtual Hangouts:** A Collaborative Approach to Reinforcing Training

CASE STUDY

An IT service provider with teams spread around the country faced a challenge common to many large organizations—how to keep their dispersed employees connected to the core training long after the initial session had concluded. Their solution was to host regular online follow-up sessions where employees would reconvene to discuss, debate, and deepen their understanding of the training material. These informal, scheduled sessions provided a platform for employees to ask questions, get support, and collaborate on applying their training in creative ways.

Trainees didn't have to attend the sessions, but many did, and they saw good results. The application of training in practical scenarios increased significantly. Plus, the live events became more than just a means of reinforcing the training. They helped forge connections between people in different locations around the world, improving collaboration within their network.

FOLLOW-UP SESSIONS

REINFORCING LEARNING THROUGH SCHEDULED REVISITS

THIS METHOD INVOLVES ADDITIONAL SESSIONS in the weeks or months following the primary training event to serve as checkpoints, offering trainees the opportunity to review, clarify doubts, and delve deeper into the subject matter. Various formats are available, repeating parts of the training, open Q&A sessions, scenario and case study analysis, and more. By providing structured checkpoints along this journey, trainers ensure that trainees remain on the right path, continuously refining their understanding and application of the training content.

1. **Scheduling:** When planning the initial training, schedule one or more follow-up sessions in addition to the main event. These could be a few weeks to a few months apart, depending on the complexity of the training content and the needs of the trainees.
2. **Feedback Collection:** Prior to the follow-up session, gather feedback from trainees about their experiences since the training. Understand the challenges they've faced, areas where they feel confident, and topics they'd like to revisit.
3. **Session Design:** Design the follow-up session based on the feedback received. While part of the session should be dedicated to revisiting key concepts from the initial training, there should also be room to address specific challenges or questions raised by trainees.

4. **Interactive Format:** Make the follow-up sessions highly interactive. Encourage discussions, group activities, and real-world problem-solving. This ensures trainees are actively engaged and not just passively receiving information.
5. **Real-World Application:** Discuss real-world applications of the training content. Allow trainees to share their experiences, successes, and challenges, fostering a collaborative learning environment.
6. **Continuous Learning Resources:** Provide additional resources during these sessions, such as articles, videos, or tools that can aid in further learning and application.

CREATING AND IMPLEMENTING "FOLLOW-UP SESSIONS" METHOD

Step 1 – Initial Planning: During the design phase of the main training, plan for follow-up sessions. Decide on the number and frequency based on the training's complexity and duration.

Step 2 – Communicate the Plan: Inform trainees about the scheduled follow-up sessions during the initial training. Emphasize the importance and benefits of these sessions to ensure commitment.

Step 3 – Collect Feedback: A week or two before the scheduled follow-up session, send out surveys or feedback forms to trainees. Ask about their experiences, challenges, and specific topics they'd like to revisit.

Step 4 – Design the Follow-Up Session: Based on the feedback received, design the content and structure of the follow-up session. Ensure it's a mix of review, addressing challenges, and exploring advanced concepts.

Step 5 – Prepare Materials: Gather or create any additional materials or resources needed for the session. This could include handouts, multimedia presentations, or interactive tools.

Step 6 – Facilitate Interactive Discussions: During the session, encourage trainees to share their experiences. Foster an environment where they feel comfortable discussing challenges and successes.

Step 7 – Incorporate Practical Exercises: Use real-world scenarios or case studies to allow trainees to apply their knowledge. This enhances understanding and showcases practical applications.

Step 8 – Provide Additional Resources: Share supplementary resources like articles, videos, or tools that can aid trainees in their continuous learning journey.

Step 9 – Document Key Takeaways: At the end of the session, summarize key points discussed and any action items. This provides trainees with a clear reference for future reflection.

Step 10 – Schedule the Next Session: If there are additional follow-up sessions planned, remind trainees of the date and time. If not, consider scheduling one based on the needs and feedback of the trainees.

FEATURES OF THE TECHNIQUE

Type	Event
Frequency	Recurring
Timing	Over time after the training
Pacing	Scheduled
Real-Time Trainer Input	Yes
Participation	Group
Automation	No
Client Facilitation	Optional
Live Event	Yes
Specialist Tools Needed	No

ONGOING SUPPORT

CONTINUOUS LEARNING THROUGH IMMEDIATE ASSISTANCE

PROVIDE TRAINEES DIRECT ACCESS TO expertise and guidance even after the formal training sessions have concluded. Offer a hotline or a dedicated coach who can be approached when participants face challenges or need clarification on certain techniques, bridging the gap between formal training sessions and real-world application. Participants are assured of a safety net, allowing them to confidently apply their new knowledge and skills without the fear of making irreversible mistakes or falling back into old habits.

1. **Establishment of Support Channels:** Depending on the organization's resources and the number of trainees, a hotline (phone, chat, or email) can be set up, or specific coaches can be assigned to groups or individuals. This channel is dedicated exclusively to addressing post-training queries and challenges.
2. **Availability Schedule:** While some hotlines might operate during all working hours, dedicated coaches would typically have specific hours during which they are available. This schedule should be communicated clearly to all participants.

3. **Prompt Response:** The essence of this method lies in providing timely support. Whether it's through immediate hotline assistance or a guaranteed response time from a coach, participants should know they won't be left hanging.
4. **Documentation:** Every interaction or query should be documented. This not only helps in tracking common challenges faced by trainees but also aids in refining future training sessions.

CREATING AND IMPLEMENTING "ONGOING SUPPORT" METHOD

Step 1 – Assess Needs and Resources: Review the training content to identify potential areas where participants might need post-training support. Determine the resources available, such as the number of coaches or experts, and the technology needed for a hotline.

Step 2 – Define the Support Structure: Decide whether you'll offer a hotline, dedicated coaches, or both. If using coaches, determine if they'll be assigned to specific individuals, groups, or be available on a first-come, first-served basis.

Step 3 – Set Up the Infrastructure: For a hotline: Establish a dedicated phone line or digital platform (like a chat service). Ensure it's staffed during specified hours.

For coaches: Create a system for trainees to schedule sessions or ask questions. This could be through email, a booking platform, or an internal messaging system.

Step 4 – Communicate Availability: Clearly inform participants about the support options available, how to access them, and the hours of availability. Provide any necessary contact details, platform links, or scheduling tools.

Step 5 – Establish a Response Protocol: Ensure that all queries receive a timely response. Define what "timely" means (e.g., within 24 hours). For complex issues that can't be resolved immediately, provide a timeframe for resolution.

Step 6 – Document Interactions: Create a system for logging all interactions, including the nature of the query, the advice given, and any follow-up actions. This documentation will be invaluable for refining the training program and understanding common challenges.

Step 7 – Continuous Training for Support Staff: Ensure that those providing support (whether hotline staff or coaches) are kept up-to-date with any changes in the training content or methodologies. Offer them regular training sessions to refine their support skills.

Step 8 – Promote the Support System: Continuously remind participants of the support available to them. This can be done through regular emails, reminders in company meetings, or digital notifications. Encourage them to make use of the system whenever they face challenges.

Step 9 – Review and Expand: As the training program evolves, the support system should too. Periodically review the entire system to see if it meets the current needs. Consider expanding the support options if the demand is high or if there are areas not currently covered.

FEATURES OF THE TECHNIQUE

Type	Other
Frequency	Ongoing
Timing	Over time after the training
Pacing	Scheduled
Real-Time Trainer Input	Yes
Participation	Individual
Automation	Partial for scheduling, not for providing support
Client Facilitation	Optional, but usually needed
Live Event	No
Specialist Tools Needed	Possibly if providing a hotline

VIRTUAL HANGOUTS

A COLLABORATIVE APPROACH TO REINFORCING TRAINING

Virtual Hangouts are online gatherings, typically facilitated through video conferencing platforms, where participants come together to discuss, share, and delve deeper into the training topics they've been introduced to. Unlike formal training sessions, these hangouts are more relaxed and interactive, allowing participants to learn from each other's experiences, ask questions, and get real-time feedback.

1. **Scheduling:** On a monthly basis (or another frequency that suits the organization), schedule a virtual hangout. Inform participants in advance, allowing them to prepare questions, topics, or experiences they'd like to share.
2. **Facilitation:** A moderator or facilitator, often someone knowledgeable about the training topic, should guide the discussion and ensure everyone gets a chance to speak and that the conversation remains constructive and on-topic.
3. **Interactive Elements:** The hangout can include breakout sessions, polls, Q&A segments, and even guest speakers who can provide further insights on specific topics.
4. **Feedback Loop:** At the end of each hangout, encourage participants to provide feedback on what they found valuable and what they'd like to see in future sessions. This ensures that the hangouts evolve to meet the participants' needs.

5. **Accessibility:** Recordings of the hangouts can be made available for those who couldn't attend in real time, ensuring that no one misses out on the valuable insights shared.

CREATING AND IMPLEMENTING "VIRTUAL HANGOUTS" METHOD

Step 1 – Define the Objective: Determine the primary goal of the virtual hangouts. Is it to address challenges, share experiences, delve deeper into specific topics, or something else? It could also be a combination of these things.

Step 2 – Choose a Platform: Select a reliable video conferencing platform suitable for group discussions, such as Zoom, Microsoft Teams, or Google Meet. Ensure the platform supports features you might need, like breakout rooms, screen sharing, and recording.

Step 3 – Set a Schedule: Decide on the frequency of the hangouts (e.g., monthly, bi-weekly). Choose a consistent day and time that maximizes attendance, considering time zones if dealing with a global team.

Step 4 – Designate a Facilitator: Appoint a knowledgeable individual to guide the discussion, ensure everyone gets a chance to speak, and keep the conversation on track.

Step 5 – Communicate the Initiative: During the training, announce the virtual hangouts to potential participants, explaining the purpose and benefits. Use email, internal communication tools, or training platforms to send out invitations.

Step 6 – Prepare Content and Structure: While the hangouts are meant to be interactive, having a basic structure can help guide the discussion. Prepare a list of potential topics, questions, or scenarios the facilitator can use if the conversation stalls.

Step 7 – Incorporate Interactive Elements: Plan for breakout sessions, polls, or Q&A segments. Consider inviting guest speakers occasionally for added value and variety.

Step 8 – Conduct the Hangout: Start with a brief introduction and set the agenda. Facilitate the discussion, ensuring active participation and addressing any technical issues. Record the session if possible, ensuring participants are aware and have given consent.

Step 9 – Future Topics: At the end of the hangout, ask participants for feedback on the session and suggestions for future topics. Use online surveys or ask for feedback during the hangout.

Step 10 – Share the Recording (If Applicable): If the session was recorded, make it available on an internal platform for those who couldn't attend in real time.

Step 11 – Monitor Long-Term Impact: Track how often the topics discussed in the hangouts are being applied in the workplace. Assess the overall impact of the hangouts on participants' performance and retention of training content.

FEATURES OF THE TECHNIQUE

Type	Event
Frequency	Recurring
Timing	Over time after the training
Pacing	Scheduled
Real-Time Trainer Input	Yes
Participation	Group
Automation	No
Client Facilitation	Optional
Live Event	Yes
Specialist Tools Needed	Yes

SELF-PACED

NOT EVERYTHING HAS TO RUN on a schedule, especially when we all absorb and apply new knowledge at a different rate. Plus, the pace of work often means flexibility is not just a preference but a necessity. This section outlines options for self-paced learning methods that provide each learner with the tools to engage with training material at their own pace and on their own terms.

These methods require little to no live support from the trainer. Much like the reminders and reinforcement methods, the materials produced here are built once and used multiple times. They can also benefit from the use of automation to deliver the content to trainees.

To help those who prefer to learn at their own pace, try these methods.

25. **Card Deck Activities:** Tangible Reminders for Skill Mastery
26. **Digital Flashcards:** Reinforcing Training Principles with Real-Life Context
27. **Digital Resources:** On-Demand Reinforcement for Continuous Learning
28. **Workbooks:** Interactive Guides for Sustained Engagement and Reflection
29. **Interactive Augmented Reality (AR) Posters:** Immersive Reminders in the Workplace

30. **Podcast Series:** Amplifying Training Through Engaging Audio Content
31. **QR Codes:** Bridging the Gap Between Training and Application
32. **Training Application Diaries:** A Journey of Reflection and Growth

CASE STUDY

A global consultancy firm with a flexible work environment recognized that daily schedule and time zone differences made it difficult to set up live events after major training workshops. The training and development team needed a different way to keep employees engaging with the material from the training, so they created a range of self-paced learning options to accommodate different schedules and learning styles. Employees had access to an extensive library of digital resources at any time and from anywhere in the world. Workbooks were provided for those who preferred a more structured approach to learning, and the podcast mini-series was more accessible for those with regular travel schedules.

The variety of options catered to the different learning styles, and the impact was that employees engaged with the training material more frequently and with greater depth.

CARD DECK ACTIVITIES

TANGIBLE REMINDERS FOR SKILL MASTERY

Training content is provided in the form of a deck of cards with each card in the deck representing a specific skill, method, or concept that was covered during the training. Have trainees pick one or two to work on at a time and keep them on their desks as visual reminders. Once they feel they have practiced the skill enough times and no longer need the card, have them pick another from the deck. Rather than overwhelming trainees with a list of things to master all at once, this method encourages focused, incremental learning by allowing trainees to select and concentrate on a few at a time.

1. **Card Creation:** Begin by identifying the fundamental skills or concepts from the training module. Design a card for each skill. The card should be concise yet informative and, if possible, have a visual element to aid with recall.
2. **Deck Distribution:** Provide each trainee with a complete deck of cards at the end of the training session.
3. **Skill Selection:** Instruct trainees to randomly or intentionally pick two cards from the deck. These selected cards represent the skills or concepts they should focus on mastering first.
4. **Desk Placement:** Have trainees place the selected cards on their desks or workspaces. This ensures that the skills are always in their line of sight, serving as constant reminders.

5. **Skill Practice:** Encourage trainees to apply the skills in their daily tasks. The goal is to practice each skill enough times that it becomes habit. More practice is usually required for higher complexity concepts.
6. **Card Rotation:** Once a trainee feels confident in their mastery of a skill (having practiced it sufficiently), they return the card to the deck and select another. This cycle continues until the trainee has worked through the entire deck.
7. **Progress Tracking (Optional):** Encourage trainees to maintain a log or journal to note their experiences, challenges, and progress with each skill.

CREATING AND IMPLEMENTING "CARD DECK ACTIVITIES" METHOD

Step 1 – Identify Key Skills/Concepts: Review the training content and list the fundamental skills or concepts that participants need to master.

Step 2 – Design the Cards: For each skill or concept, design a card. Ensure each card has:

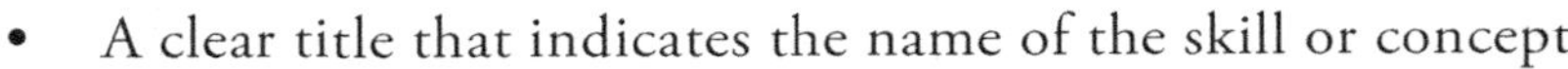

- A clear title that indicates the name of the skill or concept
- A brief description or definition
- A brief activity or reflection prompt
- A relevant visual or icon for better recall
- A small space or checkbox for trainees to mark once they've practiced the skill a certain number of times (optional)

Step 3 – Print and Assemble: While it is possible to create DIY card decks at home, it is recommended to use professional card printing services. Find a company that produces professional quality cards and boxes.

Step 4 – Introduce the Method: During or toward the end of the training session, introduce the Card Deck Activities method to the participants. Explain the purpose of the cards and the process of selecting, practicing, and rotating them.

Step 5 – Distribute the Decks: Hand out a deck to each trainee. Allow them some time to familiarize themselves with the cards. If training is delivered online you may need to ship the card decks to trainees' offices or homes.

Step 6 – Implementation: Instruct trainees to choose one or two cards (either randomly or intentionally) from their deck. Trainees should place their selected cards prominently on their desks or workspaces. Encourage them to integrate the skills into their daily tasks, aiming to practice each skill a set number of times (e.g., 20). Once a trainee feels they've sufficiently mastered a skill, they can return that card to the deck and select a new one to focus on. This cycle continues until the trainee has worked through all the cards in the deck.

FEATURES OF THE TECHNIQUE

Type	Activity
Frequency	Daily
Timing	Ongoing after the training
Pacing	Self-pace
Real-Time Trainer Input	No
Participation	Individual
Automation	No
Client Facilitation	No (but can be useful)
Live Event	No
Specialist Tools Needed	No

EXAMPLE

Here is an example of activity cards from a presentation skills workshop. The information also includes a description of the design and style of the card.

Design and Layout of the Card:

- **Size:** Standard playing card size (2.5 x 3.5 inches).
- **Material:** Matt, durable cardstock.

- **Front Design:** A minimalist design with a central icon or image representing the skill, method, or concept. The title of the skill/method/concept is written below the icon in bold, legible font.
- **Back Design:** The top half contains a brief description or piece of advice about the skill/method/concept. The bottom half provides an activity for the trainee to try, separated by a thin horizontal line.
- **Color Scheme:** A soft pastel color palette to make it visually appealing and easy on the eyes.

Card Contents Examples

These cards are from a deck with advice about fundamental communication skills. These three are from the "How to Present Ideas" section of the training.

HANDLING QUESTIONS

HANDLING QUESTIONS

Always be prepared for questions. It shows expertise and confidence.

ACTIVITY
List five potential questions about your topic and prepare concise answers.

FLOW & STRUCTURE

FLOW & STRUCTURE

A logical flow keeps your audience on track. Start with an introduction, followed by the body, and conclude effectively.

ACTIVITY

Outline your presentation's main points in a logical sequence.

CLEAR ARTICULATION

CLEAR ARTICULATION

Speak clearly and at a moderate pace.
Avoid mumbling

ACTIVITY

Record yourself presenting. Playback and listen for clarity. Identify specific changes you will make next time.

DIGITAL FLASHCARDS

REINFORCING TRAINING PRINCIPLES WITH REAL-LIFE CONTEXT

DIGITAL FLASHCARDS ARE A DIGITAL adaptation of traditional learning cards designed to reinforce key training topics using online tools. The flashcards should present a principle on one side and an example of its real-life application on the other. Flashcards are accessible online and ensure that training content remains top-of-mind and is actively applied in practical scenarios.

1. **Content Selection:** Identify key principles, techniques, or insights that would benefit from reinforcement and are small enough to be described on a card.
2. **Flashcard Creation:** Design digital flashcards using tools like Quizlet, Anki, or Cram, or work with a graphic designer. On one side of the digital "card," clearly state the principle. On the flip side, provide a real-life application example, illustrating how the principle can be used in a practical context.
3. **Distribution:** Share a flashcard weekly (or at your chosen frequency) with trainees. This can be done via email, a dedicated app, or through an online training portal.
4. **Interactive Engagement:** Some digital flashcard platforms allow for interactive features, such as quizzes or feedback mechanisms. Use these to encourage trainees to actively engage with the content.

If desired, physical cards can be created – See the "Card Deck Activities" method for details about creating physical cards.

CREATING AND IMPLEMENTING "DIGITAL FLASHCARDS" METHOD

Step 1 – Content Review: Go through the main training content and pinpoint key principles, techniques, or insights that would be most beneficial for reinforcement.

Step 2 – Real-Life Application Examples: For each identified principle, craft a real-life application example that illustrates its practical relevance.

Step 3 – Choose a Digital Flashcard Platform: Select a platform or tool suitable for creating and sharing digital flashcards, such as Quizlet, Anki, or Cram. Ensure the platform supports interactive features and analytics if desired.

Step 4 – Flashcard Design: Design the flashcards so they are visually appealing and easy to read. Place the principle on one side and its real-life application on the other.

Step 5 – Set a Distribution Schedule: Decide on the frequency of flashcard distribution, e.g., weekly, fortnightly, or another interval. Create a schedule to ensure consistent sharing.

Step 6 – Distribute Flashcards: Share the flashcards with trainees according to the set schedule. This can be done via email, through the chosen flashcard platform, or via an online training portal.

Step 8 – Encourage Interaction: If the platform allows, set up quizzes or feedback mechanisms related to the flashcard content. This promotes active engagement and helps trainees internalize the principles.

Step 9 – Conclude the Flashcard Series: Once all flashcards have been shared, send a concluding message to trainees. This could include a summary, additional resources, or a call to action for further learning.

FEATURES OF THE TECHNIQUE

Type	Resource
Frequency	Recurring
Timing	Over time after the training
Pacing	Self-pace
Real-Time Trainer Input	No
Participation	Individual
Automation	Yes
Client Facilitation	Optional
Live Event	No
Specialist Tools Needed	No

DIGITAL RESOURCES

ON-DEMAND REINFORCEMENT FOR CONTINUOUS LEARNING

PROVIDE PARTICIPANTS WITH ONLINE RESOURCES like videos, articles, and exercises that they can access anytime to remind them of key concepts and techniques. Digital Resources serve as an on-demand library, allowing trainees to revisit, review, and practice whenever and wherever they need.

1. **Content Curation:** Identify or create a collection of digital resources that align with the training's key concepts and techniques. These could be in-house materials, curated third-party content (with appropriate permissions), or a mix of both.
2. **Platform Selection:** Choose a platform or location to host these resources. This could be an internal company portal, a dedicated training website, or cloud storage.
3. **Resource Organization:** Organize the resources in a logical and user-friendly manner. Categorize them based on topics, difficulty levels, or training modules to make navigation easier for trainees.
4. **Access Provision:** Ensure all trainees have easy and uninterrupted access to these resources. Share login credentials, access links, or downloadable files as necessary.

5. **Interactive Elements:** Where possible, include interactive resources like quizzes, simulations, or exercises that allow trainees to actively engage with the content and test their understanding.

CREATING AND IMPLEMENTING "DIGITAL RESOURCES" METHOD

Step 1 – Identify Key Concepts and Techniques: Review the main training content to pinpoint the essential concepts and techniques that would benefit from additional reinforcement.

Step 2 – Resource Collection: Gather existing digital resources that align with the training content. This could include videos, articles, exercises, and more.

Step 3 – Content Creation: If there are gaps in your resource collection, consider creating custom content. This ensures that all key concepts are adequately covered.

Step 4 – Choose a Hosting Platform: Decide where you'll host the digital resources. Options include an internal company portal, a dedicated training website, cloud storage, or a Learning Management System (LMS).

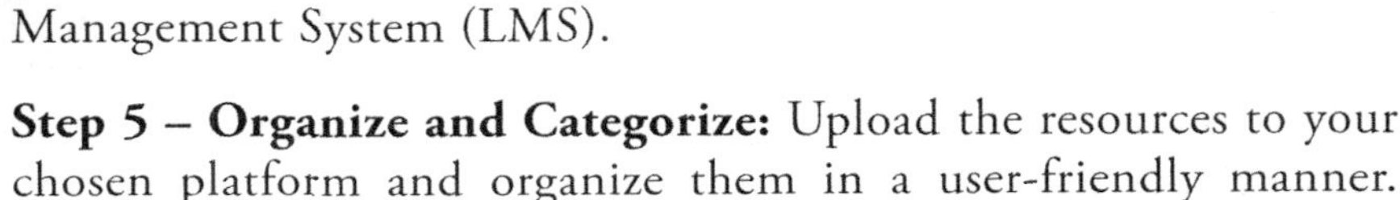

Step 5 – Organize and Categorize: Upload the resources to your chosen platform and organize them in a user-friendly manner. Categorize based on topics, modules, or difficulty levels.

Step 6 – Ensure Accessibility: Test the platform to ensure all trainees can easily access the resources. Provide them with necessary access links, login credentials, or downloadable files.

Step 7 – Incorporate Interactivity: If possible, add interactive elements like quizzes, simulations, or exercises. These can be created using tools like Quizlet, Kahoot!, or other e-learning platforms.

Step 8 – Communicate Availability: Inform trainees about the digital resources, explaining how to access them and the benefits of using them for post-training reinforcement.

Step 9 – Encourage Regular Engagement: Send periodic reminders or updates about new resources added to the library, prompting trainees to revisit the platform. If the platform supports it, encourage trainees to discuss resources, share insights, and collaborate. This can be facilitated through discussion boards or comment sections.

FEATURES OF THE TECHNIQUE

Type	Resource
Frequency	One-off
Timing	Immediately after the training
Pacing	Self-pace
Real-Time Trainer Input	No
Participation	Individual
Automation	Yes
Client Facilitation	No
Live Event	No
Specialist Tools Needed	Possibly

EXAMPLE

Digital resources from my "15 Steps for Successful Meetings" course includes:

- Checklist
- Worksheet
- Step-by-step guides
- 1-page with all 15 steps
- Links to video summaries of each point

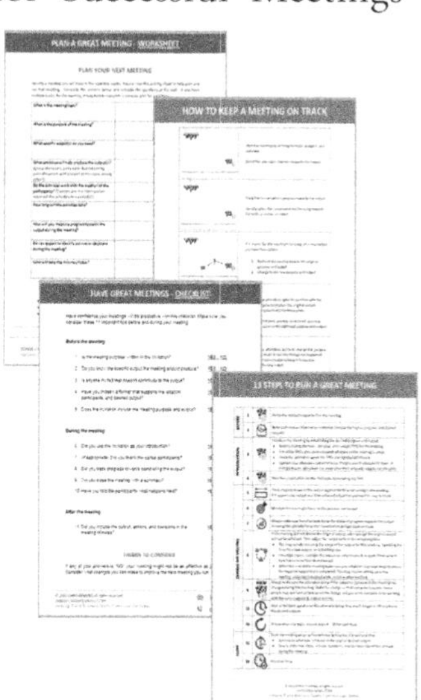

WORKBOOKS

INTERACTIVE GUIDES FOR SUSTAINED ENGAGEMENT AND REFLECTION

Workbooks serve as structured guides for trainees and provide a series of exercises, reflections, and tasks designed to reinforce and expand upon the content covered during the main training. These workbooks can be print or digital, with the electronic versions enhanced with interactive features tailored for the digital environment. By actively working through exercises, reflecting on real-world applications, and tracking their progress, trainees not only reinforce key concepts but also integrate them into their daily routines and practices, ensuring long-term retention and effective application.

1. **Content Design:** Determine the activities, reflections, and tasks that align with the training's key concepts and objectives.
2. **Interactive Features (for digital versions):** Utilize digital tools to embed interactive elements, such as clickable checkboxes, fillable text fields, interactive quizzes, and multimedia links.
3. **Structured Sequencing:** Organize the workbook's content in a logical sequence, often broken down by week or month, guiding trainees on a progressive journey of reinforcement and deeper exploration.

4. **Distribution:** Once the workbook is ready, distribute it to trainees. Give out print copies at the training or distribute afterward. Digital workbooks can be shared using cloud storage, email, or through a Learning Management System (LMS).
5. **Regular Check-Ins:** Encourage trainees to regularly fill out the workbook, reflecting on their experiences and tracking their progress. This can be facilitated by sending reminders or setting up periodic review sessions.

CREATING AND IMPLEMENTING "WORKBOOKS" METHOD

Step 1 – Define Objectives: Clearly outline the objectives you want the workbook to achieve. This could be reinforcing key training concepts, encouraging reflection, or tracking post-training progress.

Step 2 – Design Content: Develop exercises, reflections, and tasks that align with the training's key concepts. Ensure they are varied to help maintain interest and engagement.

Step 3 – Choose a Digital Tool: Decide on a platform or tool to create the workbook. Options include PDF editors with interactive features, e-learning platforms, or specialized workbook creation software.

Step 4 – Incorporate Interactive Elements (for Digital Versions): For the digital workbooks, embed interactive features such as fillable fields, clickable checkboxes, drop-down lists, and multimedia links. These enhance user engagement and make the workbook dynamic.

Step 5 – Organize Content: Structure the workbook's content in a logical sequence, typically broken down by topic, or as a sequence spread over time. This provides trainees with a clear roadmap for their post-training journey.

Step 6 – Design for User Experience: Ensure the workbook is visually appealing, easy to navigate, and user-friendly. Include a table of contents, clear headings, and intuitive navigation buttons for the digital versions.

Step 7 – Embed Feedback Mechanisms (Optional): Incorporate sections or links where trainees can provide feedback, ask questions, or seek further clarification on the activities in the workbook.

Step 8 – Distribute to Trainees: Share the finalized workbook with all trainees. This can be done in-person at the training event, or via email, cloud storage links, or through a Learning Management System (LMS) for digital versions.

FEATURES OF THE TECHNIQUE

Type	Resource
Frequency	Ongoing
Timing	Immediately after the training
Pacing	Self-pace
Real-Time Trainer Input	No
Participation	Individual
Automation	Yes
Client Facilitation	No
Live Event	No
Specialist Tools Needed	No

EXAMPLE

For the sake of space, I haven't included a complete workbook as an example inside this book. However, you can download a complete workbook here: https://chrisfenning.com/get-the-first-minute-workbook-free

The example is a real workbook I use with my training programs. It has 120 pages filled with activities, worksheets, self-assessments, and more.

INTERACTIVE AUGMENTED REALITY (AR) POSTERS

IMMERSIVE REMINDERS IN THE WORKPLACE

Posters that represent key concepts, techniques, or principles from the training are enhanced AR markers or triggers that can be recognized by AR software. These posters can be placed around the office, where, using a smartphone or AR glasses, participants can point at these posters to see short video snippets or quizzes about the techniques. This provides a constant, interactive reminder of the training in their daily environment.

1. **Designing the Posters:** Start by creating visually appealing posters that represent key concepts, techniques, or principles from the training. These posters should be designed with AR markers or triggers that can be recognized by AR software.
2. **Developing AR Content:** Using AR development platforms, create digital overlays for each poster. This could be in the form of short video snippets, animations, interactive quizzes, or even 3D models. The content should succinctly reinforce the training material and offer an engaging user experience.
3. **Deployment:** Place these posters strategically around the office or training environment. High-traffic areas like break rooms, hallways, or meeting rooms are ideal. Trainees can use their smartphones, tablets, or AR glasses to scan or point at the posters. Upon recognition, the device will overlay the digital content onto the physical poster, providing an interactive learning experience.

4. **Regular Updates:** Periodically update the AR content to keep it fresh, relevant, and engaging. This ensures that trainees have something new to look forward to and prevents the experience from becoming monotonous.

CREATING AND IMPLEMENTING "INTERACTIVE AUGMENTED REALITY (AR) POSTERS" METHOD

Step 1 – Define Key Concepts: Identify the most crucial concepts, techniques, or principles from the training that would benefit from reinforcement through AR.

Step 2 – Design the Posters: Create visually appealing posters for each concept. Ensure that the design includes AR markers or triggers, which are essential for the AR software to recognize and overlay the digital content.

Step 3 – Choose an AR Platform: Decide on an AR development platform or software suitable for your needs. Popular options include ARKit, ARCore, and Vuforia.

Step 4 – Develop AR Content: Using the chosen platform, create the digital overlays for each poster. This could be video snippets, animations, quizzes, or 3D models. Ensure the content is engaging, concise, and directly related to the poster's topic.

Step 5 – Test the Experience: Before full deployment, test the AR experience. Ensure that the digital content overlays correctly on the posters and that the user experience is smooth and intuitive.

Step 6 – Deploy the Posters: Place the AR posters strategically around the office. Aim for high-traffic areas to maximize visibility and interaction.

Step 7 – Inform and Train the Employees: Inform employees about the AR posters and provide a brief tutorial on how to use them. This could be done during the main training event, through an email, a short presentation, or an instructional video.

Step 8 – Provide Necessary Tools: If specific apps or AR glasses are required to view the content, ensure that employees have access to these tools. If using an app, provide download links and installation instructions.

FEATURES OF THE TECHNIQUE

Type	Other
Frequency	One-off
Timing	Immediately after the training
Pacing	Self-pace
Real-Time Trainer Input	No
Participation	Individual
Automation	Yes
Client Facilitation	Yes
Live Event	No
Specialist Tools Needed	Yes

PODCAST SERIES

AMPLIFYING TRAINING THROUGH ENGAGING AUDIO CONTENT

Create a short podcast series covering the key elements of the training that participants can listen to during their commute or downtime. The podcast series should be specifically tailored to reinforce and expand upon the core elements of a given training program. Release an episode weekly with real-life stories, guest experts, or Q&A sessions. This method offers participants a convenient and engaging way to revisit training content, hear from experts not part of the original training, and delve deeper into real-world applications of what they've learned.

1. **Content Planning:** Outline the key elements of the training that would benefit from further exploration or reinforcement in a podcast format. This could include core concepts, frequently asked questions, or challenging areas that participants often grapple with.
2. **Episode Design:** Each podcast episode should have a clear focus. This could range from deep dives into specific training topics, interviews with industry experts, real-life case studies, or Q&A sessions addressing common queries.
3. **Production:** Record the podcast episodes, ensuring high audio quality. This might involve investing in good recording equipment or hiring a professional studio. Additionally, consider adding music or sound effects to enhance the listening experience.

4. **Release Schedule:** Launch episodes on a consistent basis, such as weekly or bi-weekly. Regularity keeps the training content top-of-mind for participants and gives them something to look forward to.
5. **Accessibility:** Provide direct download links or embed the episodes on the company's internal portal for easy access.
6. **Engagement Boosters:** Encourage listeners to submit questions or topics they'd like covered in future episodes. This not only boosts engagement but also ensures the content remains relevant to their needs.

CREATING AND IMPLEMENTING "PODCAST SERIES" METHOD

Step 1 – Define the Objective: Clearly outline the goals of the podcast series. What do you want participants to gain or reinforce from listening?

Step 2 – Content Planning: Break down the training into key elements suitable for individual podcast episodes. Decide on the number of episodes and their respective topics.

Step 3 – Format Selection: Determine the format for each episode: interviews, solo episodes, Q&A sessions, case studies, etc.

Step 4 – Resource Allocation: Decide whether to produce in-house or outsource. If in-house, invest in quality recording equipment and editing software.

Step 5 – Episode Creation: Write scripts or outlines for each episode. Schedule and conduct interviews with guest experts if applicable. Record episodes, ensuring clear audio and minimal background noise.

Step 6 – Editing and Production: Edit the recordings to remove any errors, long pauses, or unnecessary content. Add intro/outro music and any other sound effects to enhance the listening experience.

Step 7 – Hosting and Distribution: Choose a podcast hosting platform that allows for easy distribution to major podcast directories like Spotify, Apple Podcasts, and Google Podcasts. Upload episodes and ensure they're properly tagged and described for easy discovery.

If you don't want the podcast to be publicly accessible, set up a secure sharing area on your own website or the company intranet.

Step 8 – Share the Podcast: Announce the podcast series to the training participants via email, internal communication channels, or during training sessions. Provide clear instructions on how to access and subscribe to the podcast.

Step 9 – Engagement and Interaction: Encourage listeners to submit questions, feedback, or topics for future episodes. Consider creating a dedicated space (like a forum or chat group) where listeners can discuss episode content.

Step 10 – Integration with Other Training Methods: Combine the podcast series with other post-training reinforcement methods, such as quizzes or discussions, based on podcast content.

FEATURES OF THE TECHNIQUE

Type	Resource
Frequency	Recurring
Timing	Over time after the training
Pacing	Self-pace or scheduled
Real-Time Trainer Input	Yes
Participation	Individual
Automation	No
Client Facilitation	No
Live Event	No
Specialist Tools Needed	No

QR CODES

BRIDGING THE GAP BETWEEN TRAINING AND APPLICATION

QUICK RESPONSE (QR) CODES ARE digitally encoded barcodes that, when scanned using a smartphone or tablet camera, instantly link to specific digital content. The content should provide quick tips, video lessons, or challenges related to the training topic. By embedding these codes in the workplace (on a poster or sticker) or distributing them digitally, organizations can create interactive touchpoints that offer on-demand access to training-related content.

1. **Placement:** Strategically place QR codes around the office environment or send them to trainees digitally. Their placement can be contextual, such as a code near a machine linking to a tutorial about using it, or general, like a poster in a break room offering leadership tips.
2. **Scanning:** Trainees use their smartphones or tablets to scan the code, which requires minimal effort and is user-friendly.
3. **Content Delivery:** Upon scanning, trainees are directed to the linked content. This could range from short text-based tips, infographics, and video lessons to interactive challenges or quizzes. The versatility of content ensures varied and rich learning experiences.

4. **Updates & Rotation:** To keep the learning experience fresh and relevant, the content linked to these codes can be periodically updated, ensuring that trainees always have something new to learn or explore.

CREATING AND IMPLEMENTING "QR CODE" METHOD

Step 1 – Define Relevant Content: Identify the key takeaways and objectives from the main training that you want to reinforce through the QR codes.

Step 2 – Create Content: Develop bite-sized content based on the training objectives. This could be quick tips, short video lessons, challenges, quizzes, or infographics. Ensure the content is mobile-friendly, given that QR codes are primarily scanned using smartphones or tablets.

Step 3 – Choose a QR Code Generator: Select a reliable QR code generator platform. Some popular options at the time of writing include QR Code Generator, GoQR.me, and QRStuff. Ensure the platform supports linking to various content types (videos, documents, web pages).

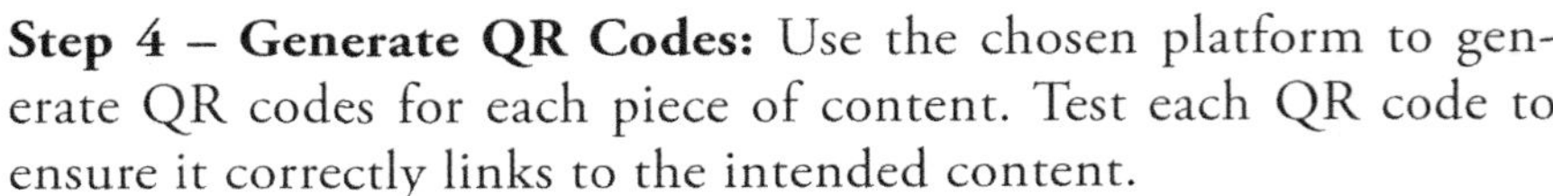

Step 4 – Generate QR Codes: Use the chosen platform to generate QR codes for each piece of content. Test each QR code to ensure it correctly links to the intended content.

Step 5 – Design and Print: Design visually appealing markers or posters that house the QR code and provide a brief description or hint about the content it links to. Print these markers in a size that's easily scannable. Consider laminating them for durability.

Step 6 – Strategic Placement: Place the QR codes in strategic locations around the office. Ensure they are easily accessible and visible. For digital distribution, embed the QR codes in emails, digital newsletters, or the company intranet.

Step 7 – Inform and Educate: Inform employees about the QR codes, their purpose, and how to use them. Consider a brief demonstration or tutorial for those unfamiliar with scanning QR codes.

Step 8 – Update Content Periodically: To keep the learning experience fresh and relevant, periodically update the content linked to the QR codes. Inform employees of updates to encourage continuous engagement.

FEATURES OF THE TECHNIQUE

Type	Resource
Frequency	One time
Timing	Immediately after the training
Pacing	Self-pace
Real-Time Trainer Input	No
Participation	Individual
Automation	Yes
Client Facilitation	Yes
Live Event	No
Specialist Tools Needed	Yes

EXAMPLE

TRAINING APPLICATION DIARIES

A JOURNEY OF REFLECTION AND GROWTH

Direct participants to maintain a "Training Application Diary" dedicated to recording their experiences as they apply the training content in their daily tasks. They can make daily or weekly entries about instances where they consciously applied the training. They can reflect on what went well and what challenges they faced. By documenting their experiences and reflecting on their journey, trainees not only retain the training content better but also become more adept at navigating the challenges of real-world application. This diary becomes a tool for self-evaluation, allowing trainees to reflect on their successes, challenges, and areas of growth.

1. **Diary Introduction:** During the main training session, introduce the concept of the Training Application Diary. Provide participants with a physical diary or suggest digital tools/apps they can use.
2. **Framework and Frequency:** Guide participants on how and when to make entries. Suggest frameworks or headings to use for each entry. Recommend a frequency for entries, but consider letting participants choose based on their comfort and the nature of the training.

3. **Ongoing Reflection:** Encourage trainees to periodically review past entries to observe patterns, recurring challenges, or areas of improvement. This retrospective view can offer valuable insights.
4. **Feedback Sessions:** Organize periodic group sessions where participants can voluntarily share their diary experiences. This not only fosters group learning but also provides trainers with feedback on the training's real-world applicability.

CREATING AND IMPLEMENTING "TRAINING APPLICATION DIARIES" METHOD

Step 1 – Define the Purpose: Clearly outline the objectives of the Training Application Diary. This could be to reinforce specific training concepts, encourage real-world application, or encourage self-reflection.

Step 2 – Choose the Diary Format: Decide whether participants will use a physical diary, a digital tool (like Google Docs, Evernote, or a dedicated app), or allow them the flexibility to choose their preferred format.

Step 3 – Design the Framework: Create a template or guideline for making entries. This should include sections like the date, training concept applied, description of the situation, successes, challenges, and insights or lessons learned.

Step 4 – Introduce the Diary: During the training session, introduce the concept of the Training Application Diary. Explain its purpose, benefits, and how to use it.

Step 5 – Set Expectations for Frequency: Guide participants on the recommended frequency for making entries, whether daily or weekly. Emphasize the importance of consistency. Consider letting participants choose based on their comfort and the nature of the training.

Step 6 – Encourage Ongoing Reflection: Instruct participants to periodically review past entries to identify patterns, recurring challenges, or areas of growth. Guide participants on how to review their diaries, helping them identify key takeaways and set future goals.

Step 7 – Closure and Forward Path: At the end of a set period (e.g., 6 or 12 months), guide participants in reviewing their diaries to identify key takeaways, growth areas, and future goals. Provide written or video instructions for how they can do this themselves or hold a live session.

FEATURES OF THE TECHNIQUE

Type	Activity
Frequency	Recurring
Timing	Over time after the training
Pacing	Self-pace
Real-Time Trainer Input	No
Participation	Individual or Group
Automation	No
Client Facilitation	Optional
Live Event	No
Specialist Tools Needed	No

COMMUNITY COLLABORATION

WHILE INDIVIDUAL EFFORT IS CRUCIAL, the value of collective support and shared wisdom in reinforcing and deepening learning cannot be overstressed. The community collaboration section focuses on ways to provide interconnected learning environments for sustained educational growth.

These methods are not automated, but they take less direct trainer involvement than you might expect. As you explore the methods in this section, envision them as part of a wider learning ecosystem within your organization. They are the seeds for growing a community where each member contributes to and benefits from the shared pursuit of knowledge and excellence.

Learning is easier within a community. Provide opportunities for accountability and support with these community-focused methods.

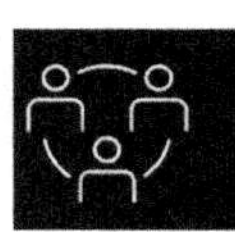

33. **Accountability Buddies:** A Partnership in Learning and Growth
34. **Collaborative Online Boards:** Harnessing Collective Wisdom for Enhanced Learning
35. **Peer Learning Groups:** Harnessing Collective Wisdom

CASE STUDY

A health provider was struggling with the retention of critical procedures post-training. They decided to shift the focus from individual to group learning and introduced Accountability Buddies, pairing employees to encourage mutual support.

The result? This not only led to improved performance but also improved interpersonal relationships. Employees were more comfortable asking questions about procedures they didn't understand. The environment of collaboration made the application of training not just an individual responsibility but a collective mission.

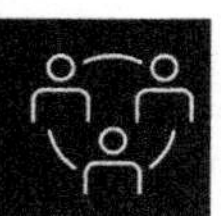

ACCOUNTABILITY BUDDIES

A PARTNERSHIP IN LEARNING AND GROWTH

THIS APPROACH PROVIDES A PEER-SUPPORT system that transforms the solitary journey of post-training application into something collaborative. Participants select a trusted individual—be it a friend, colleague, or supervisor—to act as their learning partner and serve as a touchpoint for the participant to share their post-training goals, intentions, or next steps. The essence of this method lies in mutual commitment and responsibility, where the act of sharing one's intentions creates a psychological contract. It ensures that training insights are not just remembered but actively integrated into daily routines, leading to genuine growth and development.

1. **Selection of Buddy:** During the initial training session, encourage participants to choose their Accountability Buddy. This could be someone who attended the training with them or an external person who understands the participant's learning objectives.
2. **Sharing of Intentions:** Have participants communicate their next steps, goals, or action items to their buddy through email, Slack, MS Teams, face-to-face conversations, etc.

3. **Scheduled Check-Ins:** The accountability buddy should periodically check in with the participant. These check-ins can be informal, like a quick chat over coffee, or more structured, like a calendar-scheduled review.
4. **Feedback and Encouragement:** During check-ins, the buddy provides feedback, encouragement, and sometimes, gentle nudges to ensure the participant stays on track. They celebrate successes and help navigate challenges.
5. **Reciprocity:** Often, the accountability relationship is mutual, with both individuals acting as each other's buddies, creating a two-way street of support and motivation.

CREATING AND IMPLEMENTING "ACCOUNTABILITY BUDDIES" METHOD

NOTE: *This method works well when combined with almost any other technique.*

Step 1 – Introduce the Concept: During or toward the end of a training session, introduce the idea of Accountability Buddies to participants, explaining its purpose and benefits.

Step 2 – Pair Up Participants: Allow participants to choose their Accountability Buddy. If they don't have a preference, consider pairing them up based on similar roles, goals, or departments. For larger groups, you can use tools or apps that randomly pair individuals.

Step 3 – Set Clear Expectations: Provide guidelines on what participants should share with their buddies (e.g., goals, action steps, challenges). Emphasize the importance of confidentiality and trust in the process.

Step 4 – Determine the Mode of Communication: Participants select their preferred communication channels, such as email, text, or instant messaging platforms. Ensure that both parties are comfortable with the chosen mode.

Step 5 – Establish a Timeline: Recommend a timeframe for the initial sharing of goals or next steps (e.g., within 24 hours after the training). Set a schedule for check-ins (e.g., weekly, bi-weekly, or monthly).

Step 6 – Encourage Regular Feedback: Advise buddies to not only remind each other of their goals but also provide constructive feedback and encouragement.

Step 7 – Provide Templates (Optional): Offer templates or sample texts to guide participants in communicating their goals and progress. This can help those unsure about how to structure their messages.

Step 8 – Address Challenges: Establish a point of contact within the organization to give support if participants face challenges with their buddies (e.g., lack of responsiveness, mismatched goals). This point of contact should be prepared to offer solutions, such as re-pairing or providing additional guidance.

FEATURES OF THE TECHNIQUE

Type	Activity
Frequency	One-off
Timing	Immediately after the training
Pacing	Self-pace
Real-Time Trainer Input	No
Participation	Pairs
Automation	No
Client Facilitation	Yes
Live Event	No
Specialist Tools Needed	No

COLLABORATIVE ONLINE BOARDS

HARNESSING COLLECTIVE WISDOM FOR ENHANCED LEARNING

USE DIGITAL COMMUNITY PLATFORMS TO create interactive, communal spaces where trainees can post their insights, questions, or experiences related to the training. Beyond being mere digital bulletin boards, these platforms transform into dynamic knowledge hubs, capturing the collective insights, questions, and experiences of all participants. By harnessing the collective wisdom and experiences of all participants, it ensures that learning is continuous, collaborative, and rooted in real-world application.

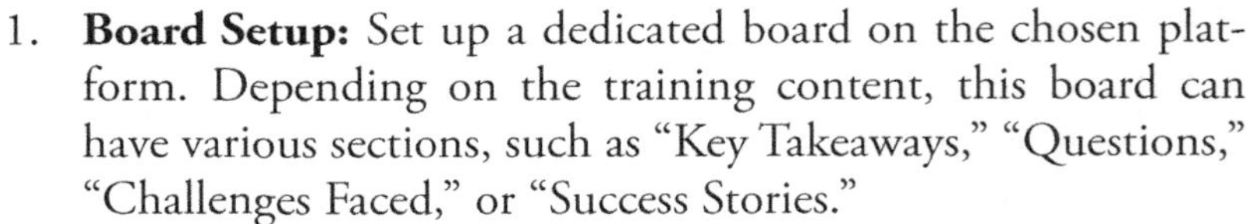

1. **Board Setup:** Set up a dedicated board on the chosen platform. Depending on the training content, this board can have various sections, such as "Key Takeaways," "Questions," "Challenges Faced," or "Success Stories."
2. **Participant Access:** Provide trainees with access links and a brief tutorial or guide on how to use the platform, ensuring everyone can participate effectively.
3. **Ongoing Participation:** As trainees apply their training in real-world scenarios, they can post their insights, questions, or experiences on the board. This could be in the form of text, images, links, or even short videos.

4. **Moderation and Facilitation:** A trainer or designated individual should periodically review the board, addressing questions, providing feedback, or sparking discussions. This active facilitation ensures the board remains a vibrant and valuable resource.
5. **Peer Interaction:** Trainees can comment on each other's posts, providing answers, sharing similar experiences, or offering words of encouragement. This peer-to-peer interaction amplifies the learning experience.
6. **Periodic Reviews:** Scheduled review sessions can be organized, where the board's content is discussed in a group setting, be it virtual or physical. This allows for deeper dives into specific topics or experiences.

CREATING AND IMPLEMENTING "COLLABORATIVE ONLINE BOARDS" METHOD

Step 1 – Choose a Platform: Decide on a collaborative board platform based on your needs and the familiarity of your audience. Slack, Teams, Trello, Miro, and Padlet are some possible choices.

Step 2 – Set Up the Board: Create a new board specific to the training topic. Designate sections or columns based on the training's objectives, such as "Key Takeaways," "Questions," "Challenges," and "Success Stories."

Step 3 – Customize Access Settings: Ensure the board is set to 'collaborative' mode, allowing all participants to add, edit, and comment. Adjust privacy settings to ensure only your trainees can access the board.

Step 4 – Distribute Access: Share the board's link with all trainees. Ensure they have the necessary permissions to interact with the board as intended. This could be during or immediately after the training.

Step 5 – Provide a Brief Tutorial: Offer a quick guide or tutorial on how to use the platform, especially if trainees are unfamiliar with it. This can be a short video, a live demo, or a step-by-step guide.

Step 6 – Encourage Participation: Motivate trainees to actively post their insights, questions, and experiences on the board as they apply their training in real-world scenarios. (See Recognition & Rewards method for ideas on how to do this.)

Step 7 – Facilitate and Moderate: Regularly monitor the board to address questions, provide feedback, and stimulate discussions. Encourage trainees to interact with each other's posts, fostering peer-to-peer learning.

Step 8 – Schedule Review Sessions: Organize periodic sessions where the content of the board is discussed collectively. This can be done virtually or in-person. Highlight notable contributions, delve deeper into intriguing topics, and address common challenges.

Step 9 – Maintain Board Hygiene: As the board grows, it might become cluttered. Periodically archive older posts, create sub-sections, or reorganize content to ensure the board remains user-friendly.

Step 10 – Archive and Document: Once the training cycle is complete, archive the board for future reference. Consider documenting key insights, common questions, and notable discussions for future training sessions.

FEATURES OF THE TECHNIQUE

Type	Activity
Frequency	Ongoing
Timing	Over time after the training
Pacing	Self-pace
Real-Time Trainer Input	Yes
Participation	Individual and group
Automation	No
Client Facilitation	Yes
Live Event	No
Specialist Tools Needed	Yes

PEER LEARNING GROUPS

HARNESSING COLLECTIVE WISDOM

Peer learning groups are a collaborative approach to post-training reinforcement. Encourage participants to form or join small peer learning groups where they can practice and discuss what they learned during training. By leveraging the diverse experiences and perspectives of peers, this method fosters a rich, supportive environment that promotes continuous learning and practical application.

1. **Formation of Groups:** Either assign to or encourage participants to form small learning groups. These groups can be based on departmental lines, project teams, or even diverse cross-functional teams for varied insights.

2. **Structured Meetings:** Encourage groups to meet regularly, be it weekly, bi-weekly, or monthly. These meetings can be formal sessions or casual discussions, but the focus should always be on discussing and practicing the training content.
3. **Guided Topics:** While participants can choose what to discuss, providing them with guided topics or scenarios can help steer discussions, especially in the initial stages.
4. **Practice Sessions:** Apart from discussions, groups can engage in role-playing, simulations, or other practical exercises to apply what they've learned.

5. **Feedback Mechanism:** Within these groups, members can offer feedback to each other, providing real-time insights and corrections, which can be invaluable for improvement.
6. **Documentation:** Have groups maintain a shared log or journal of their discussions, challenges faced, and solutions found. This not only serves as a reference but also tracks the group's collective learning journey.

CREATING AND IMPLEMENTING "PEER LEARNING GROUPS" METHOD

Step 1 – Introduce the Concept: Toward the end of the training session, introduce the idea of Peer Learning Groups to participants, explaining the benefits and the structure of such groups.

Step 2 – Group Formation: Allow participants to form their own groups based on comfort and rapport. Alternatively, assign groups based on specific criteria (e.g., job roles, departments). Aim for manageable group sizes, typically between 4 to 6 members, to ensure everyone has a chance to participate actively.

Step 3 – Set Clear Objectives: Provide each group with clear objectives and goals for their meetings. This could be revisiting specific training modules, discussing real-world applications, or practicing certain skills.

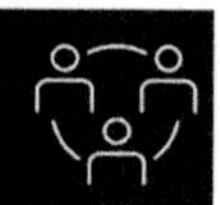

Step 4 – Provide a Framework: Offer a suggested structure for their meetings, such as starting with a recap, followed by discussions, practice sessions, and then feedback. Provide guidelines on effective feedback, ensuring it's constructive and supportive.

Step 5 – Schedule Regular Meetups: Encourage groups to set a regular meeting schedule, be it weekly, fortnightly, or monthly. Consistency is key to ongoing engagement. Provide a platform or space for these meetings, whether it's a physical meeting room, a virtual meeting platform, or a combination of both.

Step 6 – Facilitate Resource Sharing: Set up a shared digital space (like a Google Drive or an intranet portal) where groups can upload and share additional resources, notes from their meetings, or any other relevant content.

Step 7 – Monitor Progress: Assign a facilitator or mentor to periodically check in on the groups, offering guidance, answering questions, and ensuring they stay on track. Alternatively, request groups to submit brief summaries or highlights from their meetings to ensure they're making progress.

Step 8 – Encourage Real-World Application: Prompt groups to discuss and share real-world experiences where they applied the training content. This bridges the gap between theoretical knowledge and practical application.

Step 9 – Continuous Support: As the initial training content becomes ingrained, provide groups with advanced materials or new topics to explore, ensuring their learning journey continues.

FEATURES OF THE TECHNIQUE

Type	Event
Frequency	Recurring
Timing	Over time after the training
Pacing	Scheduled
Real-Time Trainer Input	Optional
Participation	Group
Automation	No
Client Facilitation	Yes
Live Event	Yes
Specialist Tools Needed	No

REAL-TIME FEEDBACK

Giving feedback and support at the moment the training is applied helps trainees start off on the right path and stay there.

The methods in this section provide trainees with the insights they need exactly when they need them, helping to solidify learning, adjust behaviors, and encourage correct application from the outset. They represent the bridge between believing you are doing things well and knowing you are.

Feedback is often seen as a time-consuming process that requires close observation to see how training methods are applied. Luckily, the advances in automation, AI, and other tools provide opportunities to automate large parts of the feedback process. If you are concerned about the effort required, take a look at the methods in this section and see how much work the tools can do for you.

36. **Feedback Mechanism:** Continuous Learning Through Constructive Insights
37. **Real-Time Feedback Tools:** Immediate Insights for Continuous Improvement
38. **AI Powered Tools:** Tailored Reinforcement Through Intelligent Analysis

CASE STUDY

A public speaking instructor found that real-time feedback was a time-intensive process. To watch their clients speak at presentations meant traveling to their office or finding ways to record and share the talks for evaluation. The need to support multiple clients at the same time meant they couldn't give feedback as often as they would like.

The solution to this problem came in the form of an AI powered plugin for video conference calls—a tool called Yoodli. With Yoodli installed on their computers, the trainees could record their speeches for later evaluation with the instructor and receive real-time feedback on their performance. On-screen prompts suggested when they should adjust their speech and highlighted issues with tone or voice and body language.

The AI tools increased the support the clients received and meant the instructor could support more people in their business.

FEEDBACK MECHANISMS

CONTINUOUS LEARNING THROUGH CONSTRUCTIVE INSIGHTS

THE USE OF FEEDBACK MECHANISMS allows trainees to receive feedback on their application of the training content. Set up a system where participants can get feedback on their application of what they learned after the training. This could be through a mentor, peer review, or a digital platform. By setting up avenues for feedback, trainees are given the opportunity to refine their understanding, correct misapplications, and deepen their mastery of the subject.

1. **Mentor Feedback:** Assign experienced individuals, either from within the organization or external experts, to guide trainees. These mentors can offer one-on-one sessions, observe the trainee's application of the training, and provide personalized feedback.
2. **Peer Review:** Create a system where trainees can evaluate each other's application of the training content. This not only provides diverse perspectives but also reinforces learning as trainees critically assess and learn from their peers.

3. **Digital Platform Feedback:** Utilize digital platforms, such as Learning Management Systems (LMS) or specialized feedback tools, where trainees can submit their work or share their experiences. Feedback can be automated, crowdsourced, or provided by designated reviewers.

4. **Structured Feedback Sessions:** Organize regular intervals (e.g., weekly, monthly) for feedback sessions. This ensures trainees have consistent opportunities to reflect on and refine their application of the training content.

CREATING AND IMPLEMENTING "FEEDBACK MECHANISM" METHOD

Step 1 – Define Objectives: Clearly outline what you aim to achieve with the feedback mechanism. This could range from refining trainees' understanding to boosting their confidence in applying training concepts.

Step 2 – Choose Feedback Channels: Decide on the feedback channels you'll use: mentor feedback, peer review, digital platform feedback, or a combination of these.

Step 3 – Mentor Selection and Training: If using mentor feedback, identify potential mentors within or outside the organization. Provide them with guidelines and training on how to give constructive feedback.

Step 4 – Set Up Digital Platforms: If opting for digital platform feedback, choose a suitable platform (e.g., an LMS or a specialized feedback tool). Ensure it is user-friendly and accessible to all trainees.

Step 5 – Create Feedback Guidelines: Develop clear guidelines on how feedback should be given. This ensures consistency and constructiveness. Guidelines should emphasize the importance of specific, actionable, and positive feedback.

Step 6 – Communicate the Process: Inform trainees about the feedback mechanism, its objectives, and how it will work. Ensure they understand the value of feedback in their learning journey.

Step 7 – Schedule Feedback Sessions: If feedback is to be given in scheduled sessions, set these dates in advance. This could be weekly, bi-weekly, or monthly, depending on the training's nature and objectives.

Step 8 – Encourage Openness: Foster an environment where trainees feel comfortable seeking feedback and are open to receiving it. This can be achieved by emphasizing the learning aspect of feedback and reducing the fear of criticism.

FEATURES OF THE TECHNIQUE

Type	Feedback
Frequency	During the training
Timing	One-off and recurring
Pacing	Self-pace
Real-Time Trainer Input	No
Participation	Individual or small group
Automation	No
Client Facilitation	Yes
Live Event	Possibly
Specialist Tools Needed	No

REAL-TIME FEEDBACK TOOLS

IMMEDIATE INSIGHTS FOR CONTINUOUS IMPROVEMENT

INTRODUCE TOOLS OR APPS THAT can give participants immediate feedback on their performance as they apply what they learned to their work. Integrate digital tools or applications into the trainees' workflow, offering them instantaneous feedback. Instead of waiting for periodic reviews or evaluations, participants receive immediate insights, allowing them to adjust and refine their approach on the go.

1. **Integration:** Embed tools or apps into platforms or systems that participants use in their daily tasks. For instance, a writing tool might highlight grammar issues or lack of clarity in real time, or a sales tool might prompt a salesperson with best practices during a call.
2. **Automated Analysis:** As participants work, the tool continuously analyses their actions, comparing them against best practices or the principles taught during training.
3. **Instant Feedback:** When a discrepancy or an area of improvement is identified, the tool provides an immediate alert or suggestion.

4. **Self-Correction:** Equipped with this immediate feedback, participants can adjust their approach, correct errors, or apply techniques more effectively, all in real time.

5. **Progress Tracking:** Many of these tools come with dashboards or analytics features, allowing participants to track their progress over time, see areas of consistent challenge, and celebrate improvements.

CREATING AND IMPLEMENTING "REAL-TIME FEEDBACK TOOLS" METHOD

Step 1 – Identify the Need: Review the training content to determine which areas would benefit most from real-time feedback. For example, if the training is about effective communication, a tool like Yoodli that analyses communication live on video calls will help.

Step 2 – Research Suitable Tools: Look for existing tools or apps that offer real-time feedback in the identified areas. Consider factors like user-friendliness, integration capabilities, and customization options.

Step 3 – Tool Selection: Choose a tool that aligns with the training objectives and can be easily integrated into the participants' workflow.

Step 4 – Allocate Budget: Make sure the costs for the tools are covered by budget. Most tools will have some cost associated with them. Either an initial purchase or a monthly fee per user, plus the cost to implement the tools into the trainee's processes and workflow.

Step 5 – Customization: If possible, customize the tool to align more closely with the specifics of the training content. This might involve setting specific parameters, alerts, or feedback messages.

Step 6 – Integration: Embed or integrate the tool into the platforms or systems that participants use daily. Ensure that it functions seamlessly and doesn't disrupt their usual tasks.

Step 7 – Training Session on the Tool: Conduct a brief training session or workshop to introduce participants to the tool. Explain its purpose, demonstrate its functionalities, and highlight how it will provide feedback.

Step 8 – Monitor Usage: Track how often and how effectively participants are using the tool. This will give insights into its acceptance and any potential challenges users are facing.

Step 9 – Periodic Reviews: Organize regular review sessions where participants can discuss their experiences, share insights from the feedback they've received, and learn from each other's experiences.

Step 10 – Analyze Long-Term Impact: After a significant period, analyze the long-term impact of the tool on participants' performance. Look for improvements in the areas the training targeted and any correlation with the feedback from the tool.

Step 11 – Expand or Pivot: If the tool proves to be highly effective, consider expanding its use to other areas or training modules. Conversely, if it's not delivering the desired results, consider pivoting to a different tool or approach.

FEATURES OF THE TECHNIQUE

Type	Feedback
Frequency	Ongoing
Timing	Over time after the training
Pacing	Self-pace
Real-Time Trainer Input	No
Participation	Individual
Automation	No
Client Facilitation	Yes
Live Event	No
Specialist Tools Needed	Yes

EXAMPLE

A real-time feedback tool exists for evaluating communication skills during online conversations and meetings. Yoodli is an add on that connects to the most common online video conferencing tools (Zoom, MS Teams, Google Meet, Webex). During a video call the user receives visual prompts on their performance. Feedback includes notification about too many filler words (umms, eers, etc.), reminders not to interrupt other people if this happens too often, and even advice on improving the use of inclusive language to remove general, racial, or other biases in the way we speak.

To find out more about Yoodli, visit https://app.yoodli.ai/

AI POWERED TOOLS

TAILORED REINFORCEMENT THROUGH ARTIFICIAL INTELLIGENCE

Use artificial-intelligence (AI) driven platforms to provide personalized feedback and support. The AI can analyze responses to questions, gauge a participant's progress, and offer customized tips and resources. Rather than sending generic follow-up emails or resources, this method uses AI to analyze a participant's progress, challenges, and needs, subsequently delivering tailored content that directly addresses their unique learning journey. This method ensures that participants receive the right support at the right time.

1. **Data Collection:** The training participants use the AI tools to answer questions. These can be specific questions about particular training concepts, or open questions inviting the user to describe a challenge they face when applying the training.
2. **Response Analysis:** When participants reply to these check-in questions, the AI analyses their responses. It looks for indicators of understanding, application of training, and potential areas of struggle.
3. **Customized Content Delivery:** Based on the analysis, the AI then curates and sends resources that are most relevant to the participant. This could be advice, additional reading materials, video tutorials, or even interactive quizzes.

4. **Progress Tracking:** Over time, the AI tracks the participant's progress, adjusting the content it sends based on evolving needs and understanding.

CREATING AND IMPLEMENTING "PERSONALIZED AI CHECK-INS" METHOD

Step 1 – Choose an AI-Driven Platform: Research and select an AI-driven platform that offers personalized feedback capabilities. Ensure it can analyze responses and curate content based on the analysis.

Step 2 – Set Check-In Parameters: Define the frequency and timing of the AI check-ins. For instance, you might want daily check-ins immediately after training, tapering to weekly or monthly as time goes on.

Step 3 – Create a Content Library: Populate the AI system with a diverse range of resources related to the training topic. This could include articles, books, quizzes, and more. The AI will pull from this library when sending personalized content.

Step 4 – Launch the Check-Ins: Initiate the AI-driven check-in process, allowing the system to begin sending out its scheduled messages to participants.

Step 5 – Monitor and Analyze Responses: Some AI tools offer analytics on user performance. Review these to gauge understanding, application of training, and areas of struggle.

Step 6 – Deliver Customized Content: Based on the analysis, the AI will select and send the most relevant resources from the content library to each participant.

Step 7 – Gather Feedback: Periodically, have the AI solicit feedback on the resources and support it provides. This helps in refining the content library and improving the accuracy of the AI's recommendations.

Step 8 – Review and Adjust Parameters: Periodically review the AI's performance. Adjust check-in frequencies, content library, or response templates based on observed outcomes and feedback.

Step 9 – Continuous Learning Integration: If applicable to the training topic, update the content library with new resources, ensuring that the AI has a fresh pool of materials to pull from.

Step 10 – Periodic Manual Review: While the AI operates autonomously, it's beneficial to have human trainers review a subset of responses and AI recommendations periodically. This ensures that the AI's decisions align with the training objectives and provides an opportunity to identify areas for system improvement.

FEATURES OF THE TECHNIQUE

Type	Activity
Frequency	Recurring
Timing	Over time after the training
Pacing	Self-pace
Real-Time Trainer Input	No
Participation	Individual
Automation	Yes
Client Facilitation	Optional
Live Event	No
Specialist Tools Needed	Yes

EXAMPLE

This example is from my own interactive AI-driven communication training tool, configured to use content from my books and courses. Participants chat with the AI, asking and answering questions related to the communication methods they have learned.

The tool provides the following options:

- Structured walk throughs of the training material.
- A "choose your own adventure" style experience where users choose what topics they want to explore.
- Users can ask questions about the training content.
- Users can give examples and receive assessment of their performance along with advice on how to improve.

This generative AI tool is provided by https://heynovo.ai/.

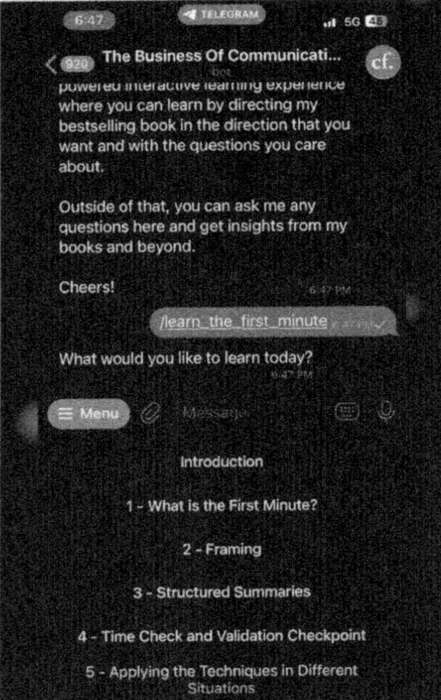

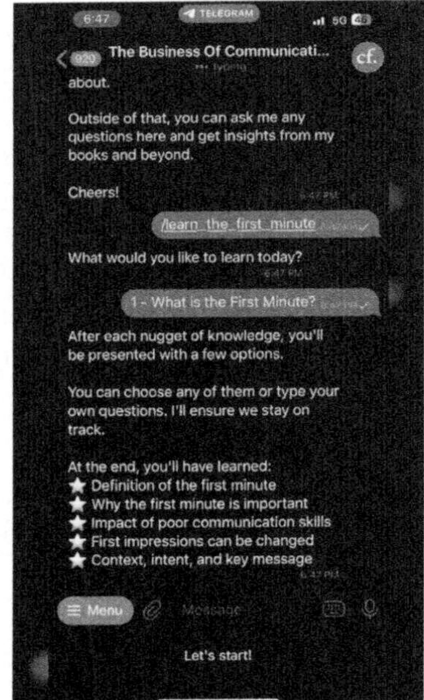

CUSTOMIZED SOLUTIONS

THE LAST KEY PIECE IN our mosaic of post-training support strategies is the art of customized solutions. Not every situation can use a prepared solution. Sometimes you'll need to create a custom solution to align with specific organizational needs, learning styles, and performance goals.

Custom solutions can be large or small. They may include some of the methods described in this book, or they may be unique, created for a specific situation and client. Whatever the approach, the goal is the same—tailored reinforcement for optimal training outcomes.

39. **Custom Follow-Up:** Tailored Reinforcement for Optimal Training Outcomes

CASE STUDY

A large defense company ran a half-year training program for senior managers on the path to the executive level. The company struggled to promote from within their ranks because of a lack of leadership skills.

To support the structured training, the learning and development team built a support program to fit the diverse range of topics as well as the different levels of support people in the program needed. The program included a blend of self-paced learning, activities, and collaboration. Some participants received 1-to-1

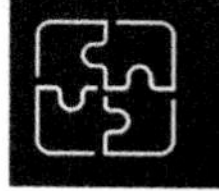

support from coaches on certain topics, while others focused more on group learning and live feedback.

The result was a program that delivered the best support for everyone involved. It took time and effort to set up and manage, but in the end, the company was able to promote more people from within their own ranks and provide clearer career paths for their managers and leaders.

CUSTOM FOLLOW-UP

TAILORED REINFORCEMENT FOR OPTIMAL TRAINING OUTCOMES

THE "CUSTOM FOLLOW-UP" APPROACH RECOGNIZES that every organization is unique, with its own culture, challenges, goals, and learning dynamics. Instead of applying a one-size-fits-all post-training strategy, this method involves collaborating closely with the client organization to design a bespoke follow-up plan. This tailored approach ensures that the post-training reinforcement is aligned with the organization's specific needs, objectives, and operational realities.

1. **Needs Assessment:** Begin by conducting a thorough assessment of the organization's specific needs. This involves understanding the training's objectives, the profile of the trainees, the organizational culture, and any challenges anticipated in applying the training content.
2. **Stakeholder Collaboration:** Engage with key stakeholders, including HR, team leaders, and even a sample of the trainees. Their insights can provide valuable input on what kind of follow-up would be most effective and feasible.
3. **Design the Follow-Up Plan:** Based on the gathered insights, design a tailored post-training reinforcement plan. This could include a mix of methods like mentorship programs, custom challenges, organization-specific resources, or even bespoke digital tools.

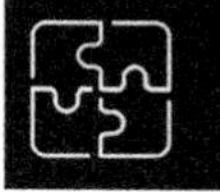

4. **Implementation:** Roll out the custom follow-up plan, ensuring that all involved parties are informed and equipped to participate effectively.
5. **Feedback and Refinement:** Since this is a tailored approach, it's crucial to gather feedback regularly to understand what's working, what's not, and where adjustments are needed. Based on feedback, refine the follow-up approach to ensure it remains effective and relevant to the organization's evolving needs.

CREATING AND IMPLEMENTING "CUSTOM FOLLOW-UP" METHOD

Step 1 – Initial Consultation: Meet with the client organization's key stakeholders to understand the broader objectives of the training and the desired outcomes.

Step 2 – Conduct a Needs Assessment: Use surveys, interviews, or focus groups to gather detailed insights about the organization's specific needs, challenges, and the profile of the trainees.

Step 3 – Collaborate with Stakeholders: Engage with HR, team leaders, and a representative group of trainees. Their firsthand insights will be invaluable in shaping the follow-up approach.

Step 4 – Draft a Preliminary Plan: Based on the gathered data, draft an initial custom follow-up plan. This should outline the proposed methods, timelines, and resources required.

Step 5 – Review with Stakeholders: Present the preliminary plan to the stakeholders for feedback. Ensure that the plan aligns with the organization's operational realities and addresses its specific challenges.

Step 6 – Finalize the Follow-Up Plan: Incorporate the feedback and finalize the plan, detailing the steps, responsibilities, and timelines.

Step 7 – Allocate Resources: Ensure that all necessary resources, whether human, technological, or financial, are allocated for the effective implementation of the plan.

Step 8 – Implement the Plan: Roll out the custom follow-up approach as per the plan. This could involve launching a mentorship program, distributing custom resources, initiating challenges, or any other bespoke method.

Step 9 – Monitor Progress: Regularly check in on the progress of the follow-up activities. Use tools or platforms that allow for tracking and reporting to ensure that the plan is being executed effectively.

Step 10 – Gather Continuous Feedback: Use surveys, feedback sessions, or one-on-one interviews to gather insights from trainees and other stakeholders about the effectiveness of the follow-up approach.

Step 11 – Iterative Refinement: Based on the feedback, make necessary adjustments to the follow-up approach. This ensures that it remains relevant and effective in addressing the organization's evolving needs.

Step 12 – Document and Share Results: At regular intervals (e.g., quarterly or annually), compile the results and insights from the custom follow-up method. Share these with the organization's leadership to demonstrate the value and impact of the tailored approach.

Step 13 – Plan for Future Training: Use the insights and experiences from the current custom follow-up to inform and improve the approach for future training sessions.

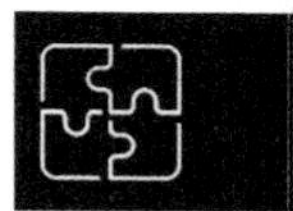

FEATURES OF THE TECHNIQUE

Type	Various
Frequency	Recurring
Timing	Over time after the training
Pacing	Scheduled
Real-Time Trainer Input	Yes
Participation	Individual and Group
Automation	No
Client Facilitation	Yes
Live Event	Possibly
Specialist Tools Needed	Possibly

SUGGESTED COMBINATIONS

Each method works well on its own, but they don't have to be done independently. Combining methods can produce a richer experience and increase the chances that the training will be retained and used.

You can make your own combinations of any of the methods in this book (plus any methods that are not listed!) but, to get you started, here are some combinations that work well together:

Structured Long-Term Learning

- 3-Month Plan
- Learning Calendars
- Follow-Up Sessions

This combination ensures structured reinforcement over a longer period. The 3-month plan provides a roadmap, the learning calendars offer daily touchpoints, and scheduled follow-up sessions allow for deeper dives into topics.

Collaborative Learning and Growth

- Accountability Buddies
- Collaborative Online Boards
- Peer Learning Groups

This combination fosters a sense of community and shared learning. Accountability buddies provide one-on-one support, online boards allow for collective insights, and peer groups facilitate group discussions.

Visual and Interactive Reinforcements

- Interactive Augmented Reality (AR) Posters
- Animated Recap Videos
- Digital Flashcards

These methods cater to visual learners and offer interactive ways to revisit training content. AR posters provide the platform to access the videos and flashcards, animated videos provide engaging recaps, and flashcards allow for quick reviews.

Digital Engagement and Gamification

- Daily Tip Texts
- Digital Badges & Certifications
- Quiz Series

This combination leverages the power of digital tools and gamification. Daily tips offer bite-sized learning, badges recognize achievements, and quizzes gamify the recall process.

Narrative and Content Creation

- Storytelling Series
- Participant-Generated Content

Harnessing the power of narrative and content creation, this combination allows trainees to engage with stories and contribute their own insights.

Feedback and Continuous Improvement

- Feedback Mechanism
- Real-Time Feedback Tool
- Integration with Daily Work

This combination takes time to set up and deliver, but it ensures that trainees receive continuous feedback and can integrate their learnings into their daily tasks. Feedback mechanisms provide structured insights, real-time tools offer immediate feedback, and integrating training with daily work ensures practical application.

Engaging Digital Touchpoints

- Email Tips Sequence
- Multimedia Messages
- Interactive Email Challenges

These methods provide consistent digital touchpoints. Email sequences offer structured learning, multimedia messages engage trainees on their phones, and email challenges keep the learning process interactive.

Recognition and Community Building

- Recognition & Reward
- Virtual Hangouts
- Teach Someone Else

This combination celebrates achievements, fosters community, and emphasizes peer-to-peer learning. Recognition methods celebrate mastery, virtual hangouts provide a platform for discussions, and teaching someone else reinforces learning.

Reflective and Scheduled Reinforcements

- Training Application Diaries
- Video Reminders – Scheduled
- Themed Newsletters

This combination promotes reflection and scheduled touchpoints. Diaries allow for personal reflection, scheduled video reminders reinforce topics, and themed newsletters provide monthly deep dives.

Universal Combinations

The following three methods can be combined with almost every method in this book.

- Accountability Buddies
- Follow-Up Actions
- Teach Someone Else

These combinations are not set in stone. They also may not work for every topic, audience, or budget. The goal is to give a starting point and provide inspiration for creating combinations of your own. What combinations of methods will you use?

HOW TO REVIEW TRAINING AND IDENTIFY THE KEY POINTS

MANY, IF NOT ALL, OF the methods in this book start with the process of finding the key concepts. If you are unsure of how to do that, here's a simple process you can use. Follow these steps to identify the key concepts for the "Make Training Stick" activities:

1. **Review the Training Objectives:** Begin by revisiting the primary objectives of the training. What were the participants supposed to learn or achieve by the end? These objectives often point directly to the key concepts.
2. **Break Down the Content:** Go through the training materials, be it slides, handouts, or videos. Segment the content into its main sections or modules.
3. **Identify Main Ideas:** For each section or module, note down the main ideas or takeaways. Ask, "If a participant remembers only one thing from this section, what should it be?"
4. **Use Past Experience:** Think back to recent training events. What topics did the participants struggle with? What did they ask the most questions about?
5. **Gather Participant Feedback:** Look at post-training surveys or feedback forms to understand participants' main takeaways, areas of confusion, or what they found most valuable. This feedback can provide insights into what concepts resonated most and which ones need reinforcement.

6. **Prioritize Concepts:** Not all concepts will need equal emphasis in follow-up activities. Prioritize based on importance to the training objectives, participant feedback, and areas that were challenging for participants.
7. **Repackage Key Concepts:** Convert these concepts into bite-sized pieces suitable for follow-up. This could be in the form of any method described in this book.

Remember, the goal of these follow-up activities is to reinforce learning, address any areas of confusion, and ensure that the training translates into real-world application. By systematically identifying and repackaging key concepts, you can significantly enhance the long-term impact of your training programs.

ABOUT THE AUTHOR

CHRIS FENNING IS A BUSINESS communication skills instructor and author. His practical methods are used in organizations like Google and NATO and have appeared in the *Harvard Business Review.* It is this experience, teaching and training around the world, that showed Chris the benefits of continuing the learning beyond the initial training session. He uses many of the methods in this book with his clients. Chris is also the author of multiple award-winning books, including *The First Minute*, which has been translated into 15 languages. When he isn't working, you can find him walking in the hills and mountains of Europe with his wife and daughter. Find out how Chris can help you at www.chrisfenning.com

ACKNOWLEDGMENTS

THE LIST OF METHODS IN this book includes ideas and approaches from some of the best trainers out there. By reading this book, you are benefiting from the wisdom and experience of many fine people. I owe a huge thank you to each of the following people for contributing to this book:

Chris Littlefield

Candela Iglesias

Laura A. Gaines

Sher Downing

Deborah Grayson Riegel

All of them are members of the Recognized Expert Group set up by Dorie Clark. This wonderful community of experts helps raise the bar for quality in training, coaching, and much, much more.

In addition, a gang of beta readers reviewed and refined the methods. The content of this book is better because of the time and input from:

Steve Shelton

Yasmina Khelifi

Heather Torretta

Julia Phelan

And finally, to all the trainees who experienced (endured?) some of these methods as I learned to make them better, thank you. Your feedback has shaped this book and will help many more trainees in the future.

Printed in Great Britain
by Amazon